Teaching **Dave**

Memories from 50 Years in Full-Time Education

To Pip and Julian

Good mates from God's Own County!

With love and best wishes,

Dave

Dave Matthews

Grosvenor House
Publishing Limited

The right of Dave Matthews to be identified as the author of this
work has been asserted in accordance with Section 78
of the Copyright, Designs and Patents Act 1988

The book cover picture is copyright to Dave Matthews

This book is published by
Grosvenor House Publishing Ltd
Link House
140 The Broadway, Tolworth, Surrey, KT6 7HT.
www.grosvenorhousepublishing.co.uk

A CIP record for this book
is available from the British Library

ISBN 978-1-78623-162-8

Acknowledgements

Thank you to the thousands of students, educators and colleagues during my own schooldays, who wittingly, or unwittingly, provided me with the source material to shape my recollections. The staff and students at Christ Church Infant School and St Paul's Junior School in Stalybridge, Stockport Grammar School and Leeds University, I thank you.

Thank you to all the staff and pupils in the 'glory days' of Horbury School – in particular Nigel Aspey, Dave Atkins, Bob Beardsell, Steve Chapman, Marc Doyle, Andrea Fairweather, Paul Gascoyne, Elizabeth Gaughan, Samantha Gibbs, Colin Goodyear, Wayne Harris, Allan Horne, Andy Middleton, Colin Riches, Alicia Slimon, Peter Smith, Tony Robery, Russ Thornton and Pete Whelan – all inspirational educators and purveyors of banter, who were a pleasure to work with.

Thanks as well to colleagues and students from Horbury School's successor, Horbury Academy, especially the Humanities Massive and the History Department. It was a privilege to work with great historians like John Gillard, Steve Care, Rachel France, Emily Speak, Lindsay Cooper, Dean Chadwick, Ashleigh Speed, Al MacDonald, Dan Barrett and Hannah Yates. I learned much from conversations with non-historians as well, so special thanks to Al Chambers, Alison

Crowther, Jill Davidson, Julian Harrison, Andy Hunt, Jess Jones, Kathy Roberts, Barry Stokes, Alison Thompson, Laura Vaughan and Phil Waud.

Thanks to all the encouragement given to me by so many people to write this book, in particular Karen and Richard Aiston for humouring me whilst I wrote a couple of chapters whilst holidaying with them in Majorca and John Callaghan for his very kind words. Big thanks to Ian Gilbert for taking the trouble to read the final draft – I've taken out most of the exclamation marks! – and especially the gifted and talented Hywel Roberts, for the excellent advice, support and friendship.

Finally, the biggest thanks of all to my wife, partner and soul mate, Mary. Thank you for listening, understanding, supporting and sharing the access to our computer. This book is dedicated to you and my mum and dad, who would have loved to have seen their boy in print.

Foreword

Thank you for buying*/having been given*/taking the trouble to pick up*(*select which applies to you) this book. If you have bought it or do buy it, you are helping to fund the carefree lifestyle of a retired teacher. 'Teaching Dave' is mainly about schools, teachers and banter, but not necessarily in that order. It's simply my recollections from a lifetime in education, from the point of view of both the student and the teacher. I finally took up retirement in July 2017, having taught at the same school in Wakefield for 34 years.

When people find out you're a teacher, they normally react in one of three ways:

1. 'Wow! I could never do that. I wouldn't be able to keep my hands off the kids.' This probably signifies that they are, in fact, either a paedophile or a wannabe serial killer or they want you to reveal that you are a paedophile or a wannabe serial killer, or both.

2. 'You jammy sod! 6 weeks holiday in the summer and you never have to do overtime – it's a right result.'

    This probably signifies envy – so I normally say to them,

'If you think it's so easy, why don't you train to be a teacher? There are a number of shortage subjects and some of the latest training bursaries are extremely generous – are you any good with IT?'

Reference to the overtime issue is a classic as well - I recall one particular parent at 9.45 p.m. at a Parents' Evening saying,

'You're doing alright, aren't you?

'What do you mean?'

'The overtime - you must have been at school for at least 14 hours today. What is it? Double time or £10 per appointment?'

'I get a cup of tea and a rich tea, or if I'm lucky, a pink wafer.'

'Yeah, right! Pull the other one. You wouldn't be sitting here now if you weren't being paid overtime.'

3. 'Those who can, do - those who can't, teach.'

   Yeah, and those who have to repeat this old adage are just asking for a good slap.

Occasionally you get people who break the mould. My favourite reaction was on meeting an old, ex-teacher who just smiled, shook my hand and said, 'Sorry.' The news can provoke extreme reactions - like a new neighbour in Wakefield who, on our first meeting, reprimanded me for parking my own car on the street outside my own house by calling me a 'a f**king teaching bastard', which I felt was rather harsh, but on reflection, probably at least two-thirds accurate.

It was only when I applied for 'phased retirement' in 2015 that I realised that I'd reached the milestone of fifty years in full-time education – as a 'customer' through infant, junior and secondary schools followed by five years at Leeds University, before embarking on thirty-plus years of teaching at a Yorkshire school – Horbury School/Academy in Wakefield. Breaking it down that's 150 terms or nearly 2,000 weeks or 10,000 days. I'm not asking for a gold medal, a lavish retirement present or recognition in the Queen's Birthday Honours List (although Sir Dave does sound rather good), but I thought it was as good a time as any to take stock and evaluate the past. For me, the past fifty years have been years of discovery – it's certainly true that you learn something every day, although you don't always remember it. Being at either side in the education system is frequently stressful, infuriating, exhausting and frustrating, but it also has the power to be surprising, enthralling, exhilarating and fun. It is literally down to how you approach it or whichever side of the bed you've gotten out of in the morning. If you go out with the intention of enjoying yourself, you won't go far wrong.

My mate Al, a teacher and ex-miner, once said, 'Teaching - it's dirty work, but somebody's got to do it!' I could relate to that but when he added, 'There's some good jobs in education, kid, but you and me ain't got one,' I'd struggle to agree. I'd been teaching full-time at the same school for 32 years before I decided to down-size, so you could say that even when the opportunity came to retire fully, I couldn't do it all in one go.

Going down to teaching just three days a week was (according to all and sundry) 'a good thing' and would give me the opportunity to relax in my twilight years. I could fill the time with regular rounds of golf, dog walking and charity work. So far the golf game hasn't got any better, the leap into dog ownership hasn't taken place and, apart from sponsoring the training of a guide dog in memory of my late mum, the only new charities I'm helping are regular small mid-week donations to Messrs. William Hill and Larry Ladbroke. So, rather than just let the schoolwork expand to fit the time available or resort to becoming a sudden admirer of the array of shirts worn by Martin on 'Homes under the Hammer', I decided to start to write a book, this book.

People had often said to me, 'You should write a book, with all those stories you tell,' and as the old adage is 'write about what you know', it seemed obvious that my theme would have to be my experiences from within the education system. The stories I shall tell are all true, although some of the names have been changed to protect the innocent, the deceased and those likely to seek retribution through the courts or by other means. Hopefully you will find something that resonates with you or makes you smile, and, if you are not easily offended - reader, please read on.....

Early Days

Both my mum and dad believed in a good education and were determined that I would have the best they could find. They had both had to leave school at fourteen for different reasons.

My dad, Percy, was one of three children brought up by his mother alone, after his dad had died of influenza, shortly after the end of the First World War, when my father was a young boy. He had to leave school as soon as he could to start earning money to support the family. When he started work in 1929, they lived close to Wormwood Scrubs prison in West London and every penny he earned was vital. He did a number of jobs before joining Unilever and gaining his education from experience. He did well and even moved to the posher part of Erconwald Street in East Acton, at least 400 yards now from the prison. He was called up to fight in World War 2 and after basic training, was sent out to Burma. He was to become part of General Slim's 'Forgotten Army' and experience jungle warfare. Growing up I can remember clearly his reluctance to talk about this part of his life, but I can remember too being woken up by him shouting out in his vivid nightmares in the early hours of the morning, thirty years after the event. The morning after the night before, my mum would say, 'The snipers were in the trees again last night.'

The one thing my dad did tell me were the tricks the Japanese used to play, by broadcasting weird music in the jungle at all hours of the day and night, with Tokyo Rose telling all the Tommies that they needed to surrender as the war was already over and their wives and children would all die unless they did. His platoon managed to hold out against this psychological warfare and somehow survived on their meagre rations, helped out by occasional air drops of tinned bully beef (corned beef). The soldiers used to bury them to stop them falling into enemy hands and then, according to dad, promptly forgot where they'd hidden them. They grew to hate the bully beef anyway, as sometimes they opened the tin up to find the meat a strange green colour – although later in the war they were able to swap them with the Americans, who were equally fed up with their considerably larger tins of Spam; so much so that at the height of the barter, the rate was one tin of corned beef for four tins of Spam. Incidentally, which state of America eats more tins of Spam for head of population than any other? It's a cracking question for a quiz night. Have a think about it and I'll tell you at the end of the chapter.

My mum, Betty, was ten years younger than my dad. She was a bit of a scholar at her Essex grammar school and hoped to move onto university afterwards. Unfortunately for her, she was only thirteen when World War Two broke out and she and her younger sister, Beryl, were evacuated with their entire school to Bedford. The best part of a year of misery and separation from their parents was ended when their mum and dad cycled to Bedford (about 70 miles) to take their girls back to London, as the 'Phoney War' suggested that the wholesale evacuation had been a massive over-reaction.

They were back in London two full days before the Blitz began. My grandfather had decided that for Betty, further full-time education was unnecessary ('there's a war on – you know.'). He decided that she would have to forget those dreams of university – she was hoping for Cambridge – as she would be much better off in full-time employment. Still only fourteen, she secured a job in the accounts department of the gas company where she would work five full days a week and every other Saturday. This was still not enough for my grandfather who insisted that she did voluntary work five nights a week to 'keep busy'. Accordingly, she worked two nights a week at a local hospital, where one of her tasks was to wash the dead bodies – they were getting a steady supply from the bombings of the Blitz. Sometimes she was even asked to help piece together bodies from assembled body parts (What do I do with this spare leg?). For the other three nights, she reported to the air raid patrol wardens where she acted as a sort of 'bomb spotter.' Whilst the majority of Londoners were safe in their shelters, Betty would get on a bike, wearing her own clothes (but with the addition of a steel helmet and ARP armband) and cycle round her patch looking for bombs as they fell. She was provided with a pocket book and two steel buckets, one filled with water and the other, sand. When she found an unexploded bomb, she was to look at its shape, condition and even serial number and, with the help of the pocket book, decide whether to pour over sand, water or leave well alone. Every few hours she would return to base to hand over her information, which would then be relayed to the bomb squad to determine further action. Some education for a fourteen year old!

So with my mum and dad both having to give up their education at fourteen, they were determined that their only son would get the best education they could find. As a result, as soon as I was born in Cheltenham, Gloucestershire, my name was put down for the prestigious Cheltenham Gentlemen's College. This would be a great start to my education and would make Oxbridge more of a reality. But 'the best laid schemes o' mice an' men gang aft a'gley' as Robbie Burns so rightly said and my dad's posting to the frozen north of England was to change everything.

Out of all of the postings in the Unilever Empire, my dad got Hyde. At the time all we knew about the place was that it had a football club who had suffered the greatest ever defeat in first-class football in England in 1887, when they lost to Preston North End 26-0 in the first round of the F. A. Cup. Little were we to know that it would soon become Manchester's Murder Quarter with the arrest of the Moors' Murderers shortly after our arrival and then the killing spree of Dr Harold Shipman who murdered over 200 of his patients before his arrest in 1998. To us, Hyde meant a good market, the cinema and the dreaded trip to the dentist, but more importantly, the headquarters of Total Refrigeration Limited. This was a joint venture between Wall's and Lyons Maid Ice Cream Companies in an attempt to streamline the manufacture and distribution of freezers for the blossoming ice cream trade, and the location of my dad's big promotion.

Although the works were in Godley in Hyde, my dad decided he was up for a bit of commuting, especially as he had just traded in his beloved Hillman Husky for the much more impressive Zephyr 4, complete with massive tail fins, a front bench seat with no seat belts and allegedly capable of up to twenty-five miles to the gallon. This baby could turn in any area over half an acre. House-hunting could begin in earnest and the Zephyr would take us there in style. My parents bought an Ordnance Survey map and drew a 10 mile ring around Hyde. We explored the beautiful countryside around Tintwistle, Hadfield and Glossop, before my dad, for some reason, settled instead on a 3-bed-semi in a new Wimpey Homes development in nearby Stalybridge. Within weeks we had sold our house in Cheltenham, had packed up our belongings and moved to our new life in the frozen North.

For Softy Southerners, Stalybridge was a big culture shock and our unfamiliar accents alerted people to the fact that we sounded different or strange, and therefore should not be trusted. Our first visit to the 'chippy' summed up our hopelessness. Remember, my dad had lived most of his life in a London of pie and mash shops where jellied eels and liquor were staple foods and 'rock salmon' was the norm on every fish shop menu. Stalybridge was a different world and so on one Friday tea-time, shortly after moving in, Dad found himself in a busy fish and chip shop and naturally tried to order his 'usual.' The conversation went something like this:

'Rock and chips, three times, please.'

'Ye what? We don't sell rock – we're not at the seaside!'

'No, sorry – it's rock salmon – it's common where I come from.'

'You're not from round here, are you love? We don't do salmon either.'

'OK. How about skate and chips?'

'Sorry love, we only serve fish.'

And so we returned home to eat 'fish' and chips, complete with 'mushy peas', which came as even more of a culture shock for my mum, but became one of my all-time favourites. To me, embracing the foods of a region is part of your education and acceptance into an area and mushy peas are no exception. A few years ago some Texans stayed at my house on the Yorkshire section of a choir tour of the UK and after an evening performance, were fed pie and peas at the local church. They could not get their heads around the combination of the two. According to Texan Todd,

'The pie – that was really great and then the peas with the mint sauce were awesome. But together......?'

My favourite reaction came when a trainee teacher from Spain sampled them at a Stalybridge Celtic match. We had taken her on the train from Huddersfield on a 'Rail-Ale' Stalyvegas excursion which included a visit to the famous 'Buffet Bar' at Stalybridge Station for a 'few pints' before the game. On arrival at the stadium, ready for some fodder to soak up the ale, we introduced her to the delights of meat and potato pie and peas and she was blown away. At half time, she announced that she wanted more of the same and I joined her in the queue. When she reached the counter, she addressed the vendor in her thick Andalusian accent,

'Two pies peas wiz hgravy, please'

He looked at me and bawled, 'Is she taking the f***king piss?'

'No, she's Spanish.' I replied

'Oh! Sorry, love. No offence.'

That's Stalybridge hospitality for you. Once they realise that you are genuine and are trying to fit in, they're fine with you. We soon made friends on and off the estate in Stalybridge and before long, it was time for me to begin my formal education.

My first school, Christ Church Infants, has long since closed down, but the building now houses a small independent senior school. I looked at the results of a recent OFSTED inspection and was interested to see that PE lessons have to be at the end of the day, so that children can go straight home afterwards, as there are not enough facilities at the school to allow them to shower. Not much has changed then.

My first day at Christ Church was one I had looked forward to for some time. I knew that I'd be joining with my pal Dennis from the next street and hoped that we would be allowed to sit together or at least be in the same class. Our mums took us on the bus from the estate into the centre of Stalybridge and we walked the final few hundred yards to the school. The school was built on the side of a hill and I can remember having to climb about three sets of wide, well-worn stone steps to reach the entrance. Our mums were ushered away quickly and we were led into a large classroom with about 35 other children. The ceilings seemed inordinately high and I remember noticing that you could only see the sky out of the windows. I worked out that if the windows were lower you'd be able to see the steps to the main road and anybody arriving or departing (like our mums). Naively, I thought to myself that they must have done this to allow more space for the children to pin up their drawings, but thought that if I had built a school, like I'd done with my Lego, I'd have put in much bigger windows and more trees outside. I had been seated at a big table next to a number of boys and girls I'd never seen before and my mate Dennis was over the other side of the room somewhere. Nothing seemed to be happening.

At that moment a girl near me started crying. I did not understand why. She'd been content to pick her nose for the previous few minutes – perhaps she didn't like what she'd been eating? This was a cue for another girl and a thin ginger lad to join in. He started shouting about wanting to go home. I didn't like this. What was going on? Just at that moment I caught sight of Dennis across the room. 'That's better,' I thought. But then to my surprise, he too started howling.

'I want my mummy!' he sobbed, 'I want my mummy!'

One of the teachers went over to him, but it was like trying to put out a wild fire. No sooner had they approached a crying child, another one started. It suddenly struck me, to be accepted, I'd have to do the same. I took in a deep breath and cried out,

'Mum! I want my mum!'

The staff realised they were fighting a losing battle and decided to throw in the towel. They quickly led us out into the yard for a 'morning break' and disappeared for a fag in the staff room. As soon as I was in the air, I stopped crying. I remembered thinking, 'I've cried like the others, so I'm one of them.'

A small dark-haired lad with a mono-brow kicked a football in my direction and I kicked it back to him. He was Kenneth, he was five and he could get me some cigarettes if I wanted some. I had arrived.

I can remember very little of the actual lessons at infant school apart from the large sand box and even larger metal water trough for use in the reception class room, which were the key areas most kids wanted to access – you can keep your Wendy House, wigwam and reading mat. All the kids seemed to be happy and the teachers were very kind and caring. When the weather was good we were invariably outside in the yard, which, like the classrooms, appeared to be well bricked in, so that you could only see the sky. Some of the older and braver children tried to scale the wall to reach the massive rusting old railings which appeared to be cemented into the top of the ten foot wall. It was usually a futile exercise, until one day this big gripper of a seven year old managed somehow to haul himself up to reach the metal. He clambered up the first few feet of railings and quickly inserted a bony leg either side of one of the uprights, surveying the scene. We were all amazed. What could he see? Was there a way down on the other side? We already knew the answers because we'd all passed the same railings from the other side every day as we walked up to school. This didn't seem to matter and a massive roar went up as we hailed the mountaineer's triumph and somebody started a 'Three cheers for The Gripper! Hip hip.....' It had the effect of alerting the staff that something was wrong and in a trice a number of teachers and the Headmistress appeared on the scene. The Gripper was told immediately to get down, but this was easier said than done. The rest of the crowd was told to go back into the school leaving the staff to work out a strategy. I think this involved summoning the caretaker with his ladder, but suffice it to say, by the end of school when we ran into the yard to check, the Gripper had disappeared and by the next day, the drama had been forgotten as there were other things to occupy our minds.

We played all sorts of team games in the yard and all PE lessons took place there (apart from one morning a week when all the boys and girls stripped down to vest and pants, donned regulation black pumps – we certainly were not aware of any Nike and Adidas at this time – and did movement and dance to the live radio broadcast). We certainly didn't have any playing fields. Lunch times occasionally involved football with an old tennis ball or maybe a damaged leather football, but often 'War' or 'Cowboys and Indians' were more favoured. To the uninitiated, 'War' begins when you and a friend put your arms around each other's shoulders and promenade round the yard shouting, 'Who's playing at 'War'? Who's playing at 'War'? Anybody who fancies this adds to the chain and in a matter of minutes, you have enough recruits for a decent game. The trick was always knowing when to stop chanting. Too few soldiers meant it was all over to quickly or it was too tiring; too many and you'd forget who was playing in the first place and end up shooting a footballer or garrotting a girl nursing her doll. Once the optimum number was reached, it was time to decide who were 'Tommies' and who were 'Jerries', or sometimes, so that I could relive my dad's war, 'Japs'. There were always arguments, but usually people were prepared to fight for either side, on the understanding that they could get their first choice next time – the mercenary bastards. On some occasions you even had to have girl soldiers – their impression of a Tommy–gun tended to be at a slightly higher pitch but they were equally adept at slitting throats and carving the tripes out of victims. The enlisting of girl soldiers would usually involve a deal whereby you'd play their choice of game at the next break – usually 'Horses' where you'd give them a piggy-back around the yard so they could do dressage or show jumping – evidently the most natural things to do in the centre of Stalybridge.

With a bit of luck, after a quick gallop, your rider could be persuaded that she needed to have a fight with one of her fellow competitors who had been slagging her off at the stables and the move back to 'War' would be a smooth process.

When it was really hot and all the kids had been behaving well, we'd be given ice lollies. I never told my dad this because I knew he'd ask if they were Walls and a negative response would bring trouble (he always ordered ice cream for dessert when we dined in a restaurant and had been known to 'kick off' when served ice cream which turned out not to be Walls when the waiter claimed otherwise). I also had to be careful because my mum had already been called into school once for a severe reprimand for my unruly behaviour. My parents had chosen the school in the first place because of its insistence on high standards of behaviour and discipline. The Headmistress had told Mum at their first meeting that, 'We aim for Cambridge.' Perhaps she had heard of my mum's thwarted education ambitions? Cambridge seemed to be off the agenda when she received the call from the Headmistress' secretary inviting her in. Was I going to be expelled? She phoned my mate Dennis' mum for some support, only to discover that she too had been called in at the same time to answer for Dennis' offence. Putting two and two together, she tried to think what heinous crime we could have committed. Had we been fighting? Asking for money with menaces? Setting fire to the staff room? The truth was nowhere near as exciting. Dennis and I had been caught throwing rolls of toilet paper in the outside loo from cubicle to cubicle before 'decorating' the whole of the boys' area and pitching any leftovers over the high wall into the girls' toilets. We'd been marched to the Headmistress' office and given a real telling off about hooliganism, defacing the fabric of the school, letting down the school, ourselves, our teachers, our mums and dads, the starving children of Africa etc. The Head finished by mentioning the sheer economic waste of about 10 rolls of toilet paper. When I tried to calm matters down (Dennis was already blubbering) by saying,

'It's alright – we were only playing at being at a football match. Give my mum a ring - she's got loads of toilet rolls in the cupboard at home and they're proper 'Andrex,' not the shiny tracing paper the school provides,' it did not go down that well.

Anyway my mum appeared and acted shocked in front of the Headmistress but secretly was relieved to find out that her son was not really a hardened criminal.

Another clear memory I have from my first school concerns break time. In the mid-1960's kids were given a third of a pint of milk every break time (it was not until 1971 that the then Education Secretary 'Thatcher, Thatcher Milk Snatcher' abandoned the practice) and Christ Church had the tradition of allowing children to bring in some snack, like a chocolate biscuit, to accompany the free milk. For some reason students had to place their biscuit in the 'Break Tin' which was locked away until break. It would then be brought out by the teacher and students would form a queue to collect their own biscuit. This would work fine with honest students with good memories, but invariably could cause havoc, anger and embarrassment, especially when students found their beloved biscuit already disposed of and only a couple of Rich Tea, wrapped in a bit of paper, remaining. The lengthy inquest after Nigel's missing 'Penguin' biscuit scarred many students for life – he'd actually forgotten to bring it with him, we learned afterwards – and made most of us re-consider our strategy. Some students resorted to hiding their biscuits in their coats or in a secret place in the playground (just like a pauper hid their valuables before entering a workhouse) or even eating their biscuit on the way to school to cut out the middle man.

All the children were generous though and were usually prepared to share what little they had. I remember standing in line waiting for a few grains of sherbet one lad was dispensing from a grubby paper bag or giving people bites of my Waggon Wheel – they used to be sold individually in open bags, were often on the stale side and would provide enough nourishment for a family of four.

On one occasion one member of the class had gone into hospital to have his appendix removed and the rest of us had a collection to buy him some sweets. We probably only raised about 12 shillings (60p), but that was seen as a fortune to us in 1966. The teacher decided that she would take two of us at lunchtime across the road to Ben Fisher's shop to buy the sweets and I was one of the chosen two. Ben Fisher's could be described as a tobacconist/confectionery shop and I knew it well. My dad played dominoes with Ben on a Tuesday night up at the Waggon and Horses and he frequently called into see my dad, usually bringing me some cinder toffee, which he kept in the same pocket as his tobacco pouch, and as a result, it had an acquired taste. Ben was only too happy to suggest ways of spending the 12 shillings and we soon amassed a small box of goodies. He even threw in a large free bag of cinder toffee, because he knew it was my favourite, although as it was dispensed straight from the jar into the bag, I bet it didn't have that pipe tobacco marinade.

The most embarrassing aspect of my initial education centres on May Day. Like many other schools in the area, Christ Church, somewhat surprisingly, engaged in the traditional pagan May Day celebrations by having a May Queen, a May King and a bit of a do. All members of the oldest class in the school (6 - 7 year olds) got to vote for a boy and a girl to fill the starring roles and for some reason, my so-called friends voted me in as 'May King'. At the time I was quite pleased and proud, until I realised that I would have to parade around the school, holding hands with a girl and deliver a speech from the makeshift stage, before being 'crowned' by some old councillor. What was worse was that I was to be dressed in a certain 'style' and my mum was beyond delighted to be asked to use her not inconsiderable tailoring talent to create the 'perfect outfit' of a lurid turquoise-blue velvet suit, complete with waistcoat and bow-tie – I kid you not. My Queen on the other hand, wore what only can be described as a full wedding dress, complete with veil and gloves, and looked really lovely. I only hope she went on to recover from this dress rehearsal and married in more favourable circumstances. We must have looked like one of the worst arranged marriages in Christendom – the unfortunate bride forcing a smile as her groom models the 'Huggy Bear Pre-Pubescent Range.' I do have a photo somewhere of this horrendous scene – unfortunately it's not to hand at the moment.

By the way, Hawaii is the state of the USA which eats the most Spam per head. Bizarre, but true nonetheless. I found this out on a visit to the excellent Museum of Spam in Austin, Minnesota.

Moving Up

After two very happy years at Christ Church, it was time to move on. My parents were keen for me to continue in a traditional, well-disciplined, god-fearing school and so my next port of call was to be St Paul's. Many of my friends from infant school had been shifted into the 'school next door,' but some of them accompanied me to ensure it wasn't a completely new set of faces I encountered.

St Paul's was like Christ Church, but on a bigger scale. There were now forty-two children in my class (I checked that on my school report) and the school building had a separate entrance for boys and girls, an attached infant school and a massive yard on a steep slope, with the outside toilets for both boys and girls at the very bottom of the slope. Beyond the toilets there were two sets of steps down to the canteen and beyond that the school football pitch, affectionately known as the 'Sandhill,' after its lack of any grass whatsoever. The walls of the playground weren't as high – on one side you could see the vicarage and its overgrown grounds and the other looked down on a ginnel at the rear of a row of back-to-back terraced houses. The Gripper would have found the whole thing far too easy and succumbed to early retirement, but for the rest of us it was a temptation rather than a challenge, especially after being informed on the first day about how we were to avoid kicking footballs over the wall. The scaling of the wall into the vicarage was easy and the drop the other side was only about three feet – even the kid with the callipers could vault it. The ginnel side was much more dangerous as there was a thirty foot drop on the house side and usually the lost football ended by-passing the ginnel and landing in the back yard of one of the houses, leaving you with a locked gate and a further eight foot high brick wall to navigate. Even so, some students were up for the challenge and one particular kid had a natural aptitude for abseiling down without the need for any rope or safety gear, earning him the nickname 'Batman', after the TV character's ability to climb up or down walls with consummate ease. If anybody kicked a ball over the 'Ginnel End', the cry used to go out, 'Send for Batman!'

Although some kids could not bear to give up on the war games or Cowboys and Indians, the sloping yard became the venue for big football matches at lunchtime. It was a massive advantage to play downhill, because not only did gravity aid you, the goal at the bottom of the yard (chalked on to the toilet wall) was considerably larger than the one at the top (between two drainpipes). In spite of this, there were never any complaints and often we would change ends at 'half-time'. Matches encompassed kids of all ages and were often very close, but the inclusion of Dobber on your team normally gave you a few goals advantage. Dobber played for the school team and was a tricky dribbler who could score from open play at any time. He was also incredibly prolific from the penalty spot and he had a lot of chances to convert them. He would usually wait until the ball was at the other end of the 'pitch' and then calmly lie down in the 'penalty area', yards from anyone. After a few seconds of rolling around, the shout would go out from members of his team,

'Penalty! Dobber's been fouled!'

The opposition would look on in disbelief, but within thirty seconds, everyone was convinced that he really had been fouled and a penalty was awarded. I think it helped that Dobber was very useful with his fists and nobody really wanted to challenge his honesty or integrity. Dobber went on to become a useful amateur boxer, but I'm sure he could have made a living as an acting coach to some of today's diving prima donnas in the Premier League.

The other new recreation to be found in the playground at St Paul's was marbles. Virtually every boy and girl had them, collected them, traded them and in some cases exhibited them. There were strict rules about values – a larger marble (known as a dobber – no relation to Dobber) was worth two standard marbles and specially coloured marbles, such as 'crystal blues' and 'eggies' could be worth a lot more – it was important to agree on their value before any game or competition. Some kids even had access to ball bearings and these were much in demand and tended to be valued by size. I remember one girl bringing in a massive ball bearing, valued at twenty-four, which was won by Stevie using a regular marble – he had to beat her twenty-four games on the trot to claim it. The marbles and ball bearings were usually used either in regular marbles or in my preferred format, 'Grids.'

In regular marbles, you rolled your marble against a wall and the nearer marble had first shot. You took it in turns to fire at your opponent and the trick was to fire quickly, so if you missed you didn't leave your opponent an easy shot, as your marble would sail well past its target. There were extra rules you could have to shorten the game by moving closer to your adversary, but most players usually agreed straight away when one player announced before play, 'No strides, no steps, no fingers, no stops – rolls on all times.'

In 'Grids', up to four players sat around a grid, handily placed in two separate locations in the middle of the playground (Health and Safety would have removed it as a 'tripping hazard' today) and take it in turns to roll their marble into the grid. Once each player has rolled one marble, the one in the centre of the grating (only one could ever stay here – it's as though the grid manufacturers were closet marble devotees) won the other marbles. Occasionally somebody would take out the grating and turn it upside down to make the grid concave, rather than convex, but the original game normally returned sooner rather than later.

All games had to finish bang on time at the end of break. There was never a chance to complete a grid of marbles or declare 'next goal wins (not counting a Dobber penalty)' at football. At precisely the end of break, the teacher blew a whistle and everybody had to 'freeze', whether in mid-air attempting an over-head kick or sat in the outside toilet. The teacher would quickly scan the yard to check that everybody had complied, before blowing a second whistle which was the signal to line up with your class, in silence. A few seconds later, classes would be sent one at a time to re-enter the school in the same silence, via the correct door (boys or girls). Prefects were on sentry duty, ensuring everybody went to the appropriate door – they were to report any student who dared to make a noise or do anything out of the ordinary. I recall once being stopped because I was blowing my nose on a handkerchief. The prefect reported my misdemeanour to the teacher in charge, who informed me that I should have waited until I was well in the building before using a hanky. Fortunately for me, it was identified as my 'first offence' and I was let off with a warning as to my future conduct.

Inside school, I was always keen to do well. I can remember the Year One teacher telling us that we would soon be tested on all of our mathematical tables from two to twelve. She would ask us individually to recite a particular table and then throw in quick-fire questions to check our speed of thought. If we passed we were to get a gold star on the wallchart for that particular table and if we completed all of the tables we would earn 5 house points. For some reason I took the house competition really seriously. I was in 'Cunningham' house and those points could put us top of the table. I would have to start learning them at once. As soon as I got home, I dug out a blackboard and easel I'd been given as a five year old to 'play school' and started to write out and memorise the tables. I even wrote out about a hundred cue-cards with sums like '6 x 9' on one side and '54' on the other. I cajoled my mum and dad to 'test' me at any waking moment and within a week, I was raring to go. Most kids who'd already been 'tested' had been given gold stars for the two-, five- and ten -times tables and there were a few others as well. Eventually the teacher got to 'M' in the alphabet and it was my turn to go up to her desk for the testing. When asked which table I wished to recite, I said 'I don't mind' and after reciting the seven, nine and twelve –times tables and correctly answering all the quick-fire questions she could think of, the teacher announced to the class that I had won the house-points. Amazingly, nobody called me a 'Swot' or a 'Kiss-ass' – the kids in 'Cunningham' cheered and all the others just returned to what they were doing.

In fact I was enjoying school that much that my mum and dad arranged for me to go to Sunday School as well. This was also held at St Paul's but had much fewer students, some strange 'teachers' and contained kids I'd never met before. We were taught about the Bible in small groups of about five or six and had hymn singing with all the other classes, with ages ranging from five to eighteen. Within a few weeks, I'd been picked out by the lady in charge and asked to audition for the church choir. My mate Rob was already a member, so on one Monday evening, I found myself next to him singing along at a full choir practice before being taken into the vestry to sing an audition piece, 'There is a green hill far way..' I was accepted and my Sunday now centred around – '10.30 a.m. Mattins, 2 p.m. Sunday School and 6.30 p.m. Evening Prayer. It was tiring, but well worth it. One of the highlights was singing evensong in Manchester Cathedral in front of the Bishop of Manchester. It was an honour for the choir and my parents came on the 'supporters coach' too. After the 'performance', we had all been invited to a formal reception, where many of our church hierarchy were desperate to be seen with the bishop (If they had 'selfies' then, they'd have been all over it). For some reason the bishop made a bee-line for my dad (never the most religious of people) and spent the best part of an hour talking about their wartime experiences and laughing and joking like two old mates. Nobody else could get a look in.

By Year Two, I'd got used to six days of schooling per week and was moved up into a new class under the command of 'Mrs Marks'. Older children had warned us,

'Don't mess with Mrs Marks. You'll be sorry!'

We asked them to elaborate, but they never did. It did not take long for us to find out why.

On the first day, Mrs Marks was talking to the class and it all seemed very good humoured. As she was telling us about her rules and expectations, a boy at the back of the class, Robert, whispered something to his neighbour. Mrs Marks stopped talking.

'You, boy. You were talking at the same time as me.'

'Sorry, miss.'

"Sorry' doesn't cut it laddie! Come out here to the front.'

An ashen-faced Robert shuffled his way to the front.

'Hold out your hand!' ordered Mrs Marks.

Robert slowly held out his right hand, his palm facing downwards. From nowhere Mrs Marks produced a metal ruler from behind her back and brought it down at the speed of light across Robert's knuckles. The poor lad yelped in pain and surprise. As she withdrew the ruler, children near the front could see his split skin and hear the blood droplets echo on the wooden flooring. The silence was deafening, until Mrs Marks calmly said,

'Now go back to your place and never interrupt me again. Let that be a lesson to you all.'

Suffice it to say that nobody ever interrupted her again. We urged Robert to tell his dad and 'get her done', but he was too scared, preferring to say that he had scraped his knuckles against the ground when playing marbles.

Sometimes you felt that the school could be really cruel, or at best, unfeeling. A good example of this would be the surprise visits of the school 'Nit Nurse.' Given the wonderful soubriquet 'Nitty Nora, the Bug Explorer' by us kids, the dreaded woman would set up shop in the cavernous staff room and have classes of kids delivered to her for inspection. The school had the only staff room I've ever been in that had a full-sized snooker table in it. Students would line up around the four sides of the table and wait to be called forward to sit on the 'inspection stool'. A quick rummage with the nit comb and a steely glare through jam-jar-bottomed glasses would be enough to seal your fate. An all-clear and you were told to hurry on back to class, but a positive sighting meant you were asked to stand over in the line at the far side of the staff room – sometimes this line also had to start queuing around the snooker table and I'm convinced some infested kids took the chance to go back for a second inspection, on the off-chance of a change of verdict. Of course this meant that EVERYBODY in the queue awaiting testing knew who had nits – and some would start giving the poor sufferers some serious grief, only to find out minutes later that they too, had to join the line. Further confirmation of the diseased students came when they returned back to class much later than everybody else usually sporting red eyes and always carrying a letter to take home to parents.

The staff room was also the venue for paying in the weekly dinner money every Monday morning. Once again the queuing around the snooker table was brought into play and you waited to hand over your envelope of cash. Teachers would open the envelope, count out the money and record information in a large book. Kids on free school dinners (and there were a lot of them) were often quizzed about their circumstances to check if they were still entitled. There were always problems when some envelopes were 'short' of the required amount and when some students needed change, you'd have thought they were guilty of at least involuntary manslaughter. Some students avoided the hassle and went home for lunch and some used the lunch break to good advantage – mono-brow Kenneth (the fag-dealer from Christ Church) was a classic example.

Ken (as he now liked to be known) had worked out that dealing in fags was a mug's game (and so 1965). His supply chain of stealing the odd cig here and there from unsuspecting relatives was unreliable, he could be caught at any moment, and the overall returns did not merit the risks he was taking. Ken looked for a gap in the market and worked out that the supply of lunchtime treats, especially during the summer, was the answer. As he was registered to go home for lunch, he could use the time to pop to the shops, load up with goodies and return in good time to sell his goods at a handsome profit, thanks to his monopoly of the market. He also worked out that his 'pre-ordering at break' system was much more reliable. He could collect the money up front, would buy only the necessary merchandise and his profit would be pre-determined. Every day he would return from his lunch break early to supply his regular punters with their goods. He always did well out of midget gems and wine gums, but paper bags full of 'kali' (pronounced 'kay-lie' or called 'sherbet' by Softy Southerners) was the most popular sweet. Sometimes kids would dip in wet liquorice sticks or lollipops to pick up some kali, but usually you just wet your finger and tried to get as much to stick on in one dip. Ken's number one seller though, especially in the hotter weather, was the 'Mambo' or 'Calypso'. These were frozen pyramids of usually orange drink and Ken would often clear the shop out, sometimes even having to disappoint some of his 'less regular' customers. Money was always returned though if his suppliers let him down and this reliability helped ensure his business thrived. I remember when it came time for him to pay for his school trips, he always produced notes from his large wad of ten-shilling and pound notes he kept in his back pocket. Everybody else used to pay in weekly small sums to save up for the trip, but Ken just peeled off the notes and paid in one go.

The one thing that everybody still got free was the school milk. This was delivered from a milk float as most of us arrived for school. The caretaker always left the crates of milk stacked high in the yard outside the door to his office and only moved them at the very last moment, dropping a crate off at each classroom. This meant that they were exposed to the capricious climate of Stalybridge and this usually resulted in the milk being partially frozen (complete with ice crystals) in winter and thick like a pungent, cheesy cream in summer. This also meant that very often kids could not face their allotted third-of-a-pint when it came to break time. As teachers would usually only allow us 'out to play' once the bottles had been drained, if it hadn't have been for Ian (or 'Big Ian', to give him his full title), some kids would have still been there today.

Big Ian was big. Everything about him was big – height, weight and above all, appetite. For such a big unit, he never really imposed himself on other students and he plodded along, remaining in the shadows (and they'd have to be really big shadows), rather than searching for the limelight. He was always calm, always cheerful and always clueless. That boy couldn't find his backside with both hands. When it came to break time however, he was indispensable. All the kids were given plastic straws to drink their little bottles of milk, but Ian never bothered. He simply ripped off the silver-foil top, raised the bottle to his lips and drained it in one or two 'chugs.' As soon as he'd done this and wiped his lips with a greasy paw, he'd be inundated with offers:

'Ian, do you want another one?'

'Drink mine for us, will you?'

Ian rarely said 'no' and if he was seen to be flagging a bit, the offer of compensation – normally a threepenny bit – would usually see him get a second wind. Nobody ever really counted how many bottles he actually drank, they were just glad to see the back of their bottle. I suppose on an average day, he must have had ten or twelve bottles, so he was probably getting through three or four pints in a matter of minutes. No wonder he was so big.

Big Ian also used to get his money's worth at lunchtime, where he became a big favourite with the dinner ladies, because he always loved anything that was served up. Lunch was served in an old pre-fab building with an asbestos roof. It looked like it had been an army building recycled from the war, and not necessarily WW2. The food though was designed to fill up under-nourished children with lots of meat and two veg, pies and gravy. Desserts were always something with custard, preferably apple pie but often prunes or a milk-based pudding such as sago, tapioca, semolina or rice pudding. Us kids would line up to collect our trays of food and then return to a table for eight to eat it. If you finished all your food and fancied some more, you were allowed to go and join another queue with your plate to wait to see if there were any leftovers. Ian was in 'Hog's Heaven.' He perfected the art of eating his entire main course from his tray, without cutlery, on his way back to the table, before pouring the pudding down his throat as he sat down. His bum cheeks were not given the chance to warm the seat before he was up and right at the front of the seconds queue. If he was allocated to a table of largely girls, he would sometimes change tactics and stay at the table to hoover up any of their remains first, but he would always find himself at the front of the line when the seconds were being doled out. Ian always said 'thank you' and really meant it. The dinner ladies noted this and would do anything for him. They would regularly slip him a few extras when nobody was looking – the usual two scoops of mash became four on Ian's plate and they could use the extra to hide the odd fish finger or slice of pie. When it was time for seconds, there were no limits as far as Ian was concerned and he often needed an extra plate or an accomplice to collect the extra leftover food on his behalf.

After this copious banquet, Ian wasn't that much interested in afternoon school. The rest of the lunchbreak would be spent in quiet digestion, sitting in the corner of the playground and he would often try to get a few minutes nap in class, especially when it was time for maths or reading. He fared better when it was art, or rather painting. Don't get me wrong, Ian was no Leonardo da Vinci or Michelangelo, but he could still make money from his art. Painting required students to line the desks with newspaper, break out the ancient caked-in blocks of poster paint and fill jam jars full of water to clean brushes and dilute the paint. Before long the jam jars were full of polluted water in various shades of browns, purples and blacks and this is when kids would whisper to Ian:

'Ian'

'What?'

'Dares you to drink that jam jar in one go!'

'No way! I'm not that stupid.'

'Dares you!'

'I'm still not doin' it,'

'What if we pay you?'

'How much?'

At the mention of money, Ian was hooked. Word would spread around the classroom and runners would quickly raise a collection from everybody in the class. It would soon reach up to about four shillings (20p) and Ian was ready and raring to go. As soon as the teacher disappeared out of the class for his mid-afternoon smoke; sorry, I meant 'popped out to see the teacher next door', the game was on. Somebody would create a jam jar mix and after a quick countdown, Ian would chug down the offending liquid and let out an almighty burp. A small cheer would break out, some people would pat Ian on the back and the treasurer would pay out his reward. Everybody would be back in their seat and 'on task' when the teacher returned, munching a Trebor mint to freshen his smoky breath ('Trebor mints are a minty bit stronger, Stick 'em up your bum and they last a bit longer!' as we used to say.) He would survey the scene with some satisfaction. The kids were so scared of him; he could control them from beyond the classroom. Now that's what I call 'distance learning.' At that moment his eyes would land on Ian and a shout would go up:

'Ian, have you been drinking the dirty paint water again?'

'What? No, Sir. Not me, Sir. I've been painting.'

'Yes, painting your face, lips, tongue and teeth. You really are a stupid boy. Get out!'

Ian would slink out, but only after giving us the thumbs up and flashing a purple/blue/brown/black* toothy smile (* delete as appropriate). I often wonder if the toxic paint had any effect on him. I suppose all the milk he drank lined his stomach and prepared him for the worst.

I lost track of Ian when I moved away from Stalybridge. The last time I saw him was at a Summer Fayre at the school that I visited the year after we moved onto senior school. He had not changed a bit. He'd won an enormous tinned steak and kidney pudding on the Tombola stall and wanted me to tell him how to cook it, as his reading skills did not stretch that far. The pudding needed to be steamed for about four hours and I explained about how he could do it and when to open it. He was over the moon and announced that he was going to run home and get started on it. His mum and dad were in Blackpool for the night and had left him to fend for himself. The pudding would be a nice starter before the double-portion fish and chip supper he was planning.

One other strong memory I have from Junior School surrounds school trips. The school ran an annual 'residential' during school holiday time to give kids a chance of experiencing a world away from their parents and the parents a break from their kids. I was very keen to go and can remember saving up and paying monthly sums on a payment card for the chance to experience the excitement of a holiday away with my friends.

The first one I got to go on was a three-night stay in London. We took an extremely slow coach from Stalybridge down to the capital and stayed in some cheap run-down hotel, somewhere near Euston. I can't remember all that we did but recall going to The Post Office Tower, Westminster Abbey (when it was free to get in) and Hampton Court Maze. One of the highlights was going to London Zoo where the teachers managed to lose one of the youngest boys on the trip. A search was undertaken and he was found at the Elephant House – apparently he'd decided that he didn't want to return to Stalybridge and would have preferred to have been left in Regent's Park, where he could be with the elephants and could train to become a zoo-keeper. It was pointed out that this was no way for a seven year old to exist and that his mum and dad might object, but the promise of tea at one of the famous Lyons Corner Houses and a night at the London Palladium were probably more persuasive reasons for him to re-join us. Actually I remember finding a caterpillar on my egg mayonnaise salad at 'Joe Lyons' (as my mum and dad called it) and the teachers had 'forgotten' to tell us that the entertainment at the Palladium that night was an 'Old Time Music Hall,' starring Des O'Connor. I think I should have volunteered to stay with Sabu and his elephants.

The following year, the school planned its first overseas trip and many of the same kids went again – even Sabu was allowed as the Isle of Man was going to be an elephant-free zone. I'd never been outside England before and so was, understandably, 'beyond excited.' We had plans for midnight feasts and on our first morning four of us got up at 6 a.m. to walk down to the beach for a game of football and a dip in the sea. We returned before the designated 'getting up time' of 7.30 a.m. and nobody was the wiser – I tell you, Health and Safety did not exist in 1971. The holiday saw us visit all the major tourist sites on the island like Peel, Ramsey and the Laxey Wheel, but also for some reason, Ronaldsway Airport. We were there for a morning to 'look at the planes.' I thought it was a bit risky in that Sabu might have wanted to stay to train to become an air traffic controller, but in the end, everything passed off without incident.

In the evenings we often went to a local park to play 'rounders', before stopping for fish and chips and the amusements on the way home. 1971 was the year of decimalisation, but nobody had told the amusement owners of the Isle of Man, whose machines still only took the old pennies. This was great news for us avid gamblers, as you got twelve goes for a shilling instead of five and could change your winnings (if you had any) back to the new decimal coins when you left. High on gambling and stuffed with fish and chips (without bits), we would enter the B and B and inexplicably were offered a bottle of coke or orange as a nightcap. This usually put some kids over the edge and guaranteed noise in the corridors, midnight feasts and tired kids in the morning.

1971 was also my final year at St Paul's and time for the dreaded 11-plus. The day of the exam was the only day I was ever late to school in my entire career. The bus broke down and I missed the first fifteen minutes of the exam. Somehow I manged to pass and was offered a place at Hyde Grammar. My parents also applied for me to sit the entrance exams for the direct-grant grammar schools of Stockport and Manchester. When I discovered that Manchester Grammar School had mandatory nude swimming for all its students, I was mightily relieved to have failed their exam. I passed the one at Stockport however and following separate successful interviews with myself and my parents, Stockport Grammar offered me an assisted place. For Mum and Dad, this was as good as Cheltenham Gentlemen's College any day.

The Cheltenham of the North

If moving north from Cheltenham to Stalybridge was a 'culture shock', moving schools from St Paul's to the all-boys Stockport Grammar was like entering a new universe. Somehow, your scruffy eleven year old with the un-tucked shirt and traces of kali on his jumper, who collected football cards, conkers and marbles had been granted membership of an exclusive gentleman's club (minus the lap dancing and urinating in the plant pots). In spite of this, I remember opening the acceptance letter from the school in front of my parents with a sense of excitement and no hint of foreboding. I just couldn't believe it was happening – I had to read it a couple more times for it to really sink in.

It was going to be so different. To see how different, you just had to look at the uniform requirements. Stalybridge was 'wear what you like'; at Stockport there were regulation ties, blazers, braided jumpers (sleeved and sleeveless), socks (long and short), shoes, rugby kit, gym kit, cricket whites (including sleeved and sleeve-less jumpers) and to top it all off, a school cap. First year students were also told they had to wear shorts to make them stand out in the school. Everything had to be bought from the school supplier, Henry Barrie, where my dad asked if staff usually wore masks and wanted to know where they stabled their horses - he thought it was highway robbery.

The two worst parts of the uniform, once you'd got over the shock of the gold-braided blazer, were the shorts and caps. I'd been wearing long trousers since the age of seven and the sight of my (extremely) chubby legs in shorts was not a good one. Older students decided that bare legs were 'fair game' and when a class of first-years were walking down the corridor, the shout of 'Sprogs!' would go up and a riot of slapping and tie flicking would ensue. The caps were equally annoying. They had to be worn by all students in the first four years from the moment they left home for school till arrival for registration and from the moment they left school until they arrived home. The school rules actually stated that the order was 'relaxed' for pupils in Fifth and Sixth Form, 'provided boys have reasonable haircuts.' One of my mates was given a detention for not wearing his cap six miles from the school gates – apparently he was seen by a chemistry teacher who was looking for miscreants by hiding in the bushes near a bus stop in an outlying village.

To show its status, the school also had a Latin motto, 'Vincit qui patitur.' I was sure this was important and convinced myself that I needed to know its meaning before starting at Stockport. In those pre-computer days, before you could 'Google' it or 'Ask Jeeves', you had to resort to 'Ask Mum' or 'Ask Dad.' My dad hadn't a clue; but my mum knew two out of three words – only the 'patitur' puzzled her. She suggested that I asked the vicar, who was allegedly a bit of a Latin scholar. He invited me into his study, spent twenty minutes poring over Latin dictionaries, before declaring that it could mean either, 'He who endures, conquers' or 'He who suffers, conquers'. Anyone forced to wear shorts in the depths of winter, would tell you that the second translation is the more accurate.

The school had been founded in 1487 by an ex-Lord Mayor of London and one-time-local-lad-made-good, Sir Edmund Shaa. Thinking of his soul in those god-fearing times, he left money in his will for the setting up of a school to educate the sons of young gentlemen of the town, with the understanding that the priest in charge prayed for his salvation. This was a sure-fire way of shortening his stay in Purgatory and ensuring his elevation into Heaven. I'm sure the school was first founded with these good intentions, but by 1972, the fervent prayer was usually limited to the annual Founder's Day service at St Mary's in the centre of Stockport or to the required choir practices of his favoured Latin psalm, 'De Profundis Clamavi Ad Te Domine......' I can still quote you the psalm today word-for-word in Latin, but in spite of my A-level in the subject, I'd struggle to translate any of it. Thousands of boys (and now girls) owe a debt of gratitude to 'Our Ed', but to students from the last century and this, Founders Day probably means little more than a half-day holiday, after the compulsory attendance at St Mary's.

By the time I started at Stockport, my family circumstances had changed. My dad had suffered a massive stroke, leaving him paralysed down the whole of his left side and was forced to take ill-health retirement from work. He was confined to the downstairs part of the house for many months and could no longer drive. The stroke had happened whilst he was driving us home from a Stalybridge Celtic game. It was a bitterly cold day in December, but we'd beaten Port Vale Reserves 5-1 and were in good spirits. My dad was turning the car into the drive when he suddenly let out a gasp and somehow crashed it into the low garden wall. My mum knew what was happening straight away. She told my dad to stay still, leant across to switch off the engine and dispatched me to 'Uncle Jim's' to get help. As I frantically knocked on the neighbour's door, I turned to see my dad open his door and fall out of the Zephyr into the road. Some locals helped to get my dad into the house, move the car from the road and my mum called for the ambulance. He was in hospital for thirteen weeks and on his return home, we started looking for a bungalow to make it easier for him to get around. As I was due to start school in Stockport, one nearer there would be an added bonus.

My first day at Stockport (or SGS as it was known) arrived and I experienced my first commute from Stalybridge. I was up at 6a.m and after washing, dressing and breakfasting, walked the half mile to the bus stop. A bus took me straight down to Stalybridge Bus Station, before walking from there to the train station. The regular 'push-me-pull-me' train then took twenty minutes to Stockport Edgeley. A walk down the station approach was followed by a hop onto another bus to drop me off at school. The whole process had to be done in reverse on the way home and I would usually arrive home sometime after 6 p.m. Fortunately, my mum had learned to drive after my dad's stroke, and for a few days in most weeks, was prepared to collect me from school, especially when I had had P.E. and was carrying all the required kit.

My first day at SGS was also very scary, but quite exciting. My mum accompanied me as far as the railway station, but when we got there, I spied several other students in the tell-tale gold-braided blazers. I insisted on being left alone and went into the same carriage as them. Most of them seemed friendly and I met another lad who was starting at the same time. On arrival at the school, we were shown into a large library and told to wait. We were informed that there were ninety first years, who would be split into three forms – 1A (for the students they expected to be the high fliers; many of whom were from the school's own junior school), 1B and 1X (for the 'unknown quantity'). This is what the kids (not the staff) said and it came as no surprise that I was to be in 1X. They were unsure what they would get from me.

One of the biggest changes for me was the names. Every student was to be addressed by their surname and never their Christian name. I'd been 'David' for years in my previous schools, yet now to all the teachers and most of the students; I was 'Matthews'! I thought it was a 'bit rude', but soon got into the habit of calling out to a 'Smith, Strange or Sutcliffe.' After a few weeks though, students were starting to get to know each other and so Christian names or more likely, nicknames, became the norm when teachers were not involved. In no time at all, H, Wall, Beefy, Salty, Diddy, Priest, Smiffy, Madman and my own nickname, Sam, passed into everyday usage.

I settled into the work and class very quickly. I loved the lessons and although I soon considered myself a Stopfordian, I still felt sort of 'out of place.' One teacher did an anonymous survey with my class about lifestyle and beliefs and it was clear, even with the anonymity, I was the odd-one-out. Most boys' fathers were professionals, highly successful tradesmen or senior management – only one father was 'retired', mine. All bar one student had travelled abroad – I didn't think the Isle of Man counted. Only one student was not a staunch supporter of the Conservative Party – me. I could go on, but I think you get the picture.

If I think I stood out because of my 'lifestyle', my appearance and clothing made me stand out even more. I was red-faced, overweight and with the dodgy shorts, I seemed completely out of place. Even my accent, a mixture of London, posh Essex and Stalybridge seemed to draw attention. In one of the first French lessons, the ancient French master declared,

'Accent, laddie! All stations east of Stalybridge.'

When I tried to explain that I had lived for most of my childhood in Stalybridge and in all likelihood, had picked up some traits of the local dialect, I was quickly cut off. I even got bullied by the caretaking staff, or more accurately by one caretaker, George.

George was of medium height, but was distinguished mainly by his head of very white and wild hair and his wearing of very thick-rimmed sunglasses. You could never see his eyes and it was rumoured that he was either blind, an albino or a vampire. He always wore a long grey coat over light-blue work trousers. George seemed to spend most of his days mopping and usually announced his presence by scraping along or kicking along his prized metal bucket. He must have smoked about sixty Woodbines a day because he reeked of tobacco mixed with Dettol and spoke in a voice resembling either of Marge Simpson's sisters. We first met on my second day at Stockport when I nearly stepped into his bucket as I left the boys' toilets next to the yard (We had inside toilets at SGS - I'd definitely gone up in the world). He stood in the doorway as I attempted to leave and with mop held across the door to block my exit, he pushed me back into the toilets. I backed up until my back hit the side of the end toilet stall and I could retreat no further. George thrust the mop at me again and said,

'Don't ever make fun of me again, or I'll kill you!'

As this was the first time I'd seen or even heard of the guy, I was a bit shocked to say the least.

'What are you on about? I've never even seen you before.' I replied.

'You know! I'm warning you!'

After further attempts to plead my innocence, and further threats from George, l was allowed to go. After this first altercation, I tended to avoid him the best I could. I'd even been known to turn around in a corridor and take a more circuitous route to my destination. I asked some fellow students about George and they informed me that he was one of the 'characters' in the school and was probably mentally deranged, but harmless. This was partially confirmed a few weeks later.

The ancient French teacher – the 'all stations east of Stalybridge guy' – was in the habit of recording a French broadcast on the radio after school some nights. He used to set up the radio and then press the record and play button on his ancient cassette recorder with the external microphone. Once the introductory music started to play, he closed the door and nipped out for a fag, whilst the thirty minute programme was recorded in the silent classroom on the top floor of the school. Unfortunately on this occasion, the over-sensitive microphone also picked up the unmistakable smoker's cough and metallic clunk of George's bucket as he brought it up a stair at a time to clean the steps and the top corridor. This was bad enough, but on reaching what was probably the top stair, a silent pause was followed by an almighty crash as the bucket descended the stairs at an alarming rate, seemingly hitting most of them and blocking out all the French dialogue. This was followed by the dulcet tones of George shouting,

'Mr Blackshaw, Mr Blackshaw! I've dropped me f**king bucket!!'

There are twenty-nine other students somewhere who can testify to the last part of this story. The French teacher never used to check his recordings before playing them and this occasion was no exception. It turned out to be one of the best ever French lessons.

The other member of staff to bully me was the Chemistry teacher. He ran the Air Training Corps at the school and had been in the RAF at the end of WW2. He still used to think of himself as being in the services and loved the special ATC days when he was allowed to wear his uniform and could play at being a 'Brylcreem Boy' (without the hair) again and answer only to the title of 'Squadron Leader'. He loved picking on the little 'squaddies' in training, but reserved his main loathing for any student who was particularly weak in Chemistry. To say I was weak at Chemistry was a gross under-statement – I was clueless. On one particular morning, the Air Vice-Marshal was doing some kind of experiments with flasks of air, Bunsen burners and a range of chemicals – most of which I'd never heard of. All of a sudden, he threw out a question,

'Matthews. What gas is given off here?'

'I'm sorry, sir. I'd probably take a guess on oxygen, but really, I haven't got a clue,' I replied.

'And that's because you're a stupid fat boy, Matthews!'

'That's a bit rich coming from you, Porkie. I couldn't see the experiment because I was blinded with the glare of the sun from your fat, bald head!'

OK, so I didn't actually say that, but I did retort with something about him being a 'bald git' and was given a detention for it.

I think it must be a thing with ex-military bigwigs that winds me up. Years later, I was introduced to a retired Navy Commander at a function. I'd noticed that he was being obnoxious to the staff and was trying to throw his weight about, telling people what to do. A friend introduced us and I shook his hand,

'Ah, Mr Jenkins. Pleased to meet you. I'm Dave Matthews, a friend of your niece, Sue.'

'It's Commander, actually.'

'Sorry?'

'I'm ex-RN, so I prefer to be known as 'Commander'. You should address me as 'Commander Jenkins.''

'Oh, OK then. I'm a school teacher. You can address me as 'Sir.''

That sunk his battleship.

Fortunately, most of the staff at SGS were not like Squadron Leader Biggles and looking back on it, I suffered less bullying than plenty of other victims. My arch-nemesis and chief tormentor though was a lad two years above me who, for some reason, took an instant dislike to me from the first time he clapped eyes on me. His name was Church and you didn't want to mess with him.

Church must have been close to six foot and had long, greasy hair which sometimes hung down over his acne-ridden forehead. He never had his top button buttoned and had his tie in a massive Windsor knot (very much against school rules). He always wore these thick black boots, which he liked to exercise on first-years on a regular basis. He strutted around with his gang of smaller cronies for back-up and was keen to entertain them by verbally and physically abusing smaller students at every opportunity. They usually just grunted or laughed at his actions, but never really got themselves involved in any of the rough stuff, unless it was to restrain, or sit on, a first-year to make their leader's job a little easier. Out of all the first-years, I was the one who seemed to get most of Church's attention. Every time he caught sight of me, he'd shout out something like,

'Hey, Fatty. Why are you sho fat? I'm gonna schmack you, you fat bashtard!'

And he usually did.

The more observant of you will be thinking that there are some shocking typos on 'sho', 'schmack' etc, but this is the way Church spoke - in a menacing lishp, sorry, 'lisp'. I'd picked up on this and had learned from an early age that I was really quite good at accents and impersonations. After a number of verbal and physical attacks, suffered in virtual silence, I had to try something different. And so a few days later, in the school canteen, the worm turned.

Church was queuing up with some of his posse to get their lunch, whilst I was already seated at a table with a few other first years. He caught sight of me and, powerless to resist, he pointed me out to his mates, calling out,

'Hey, Fatty! Leave shome for ush, you greedy f**ker!'

I stared him in the eyes and retorted with, 'Pissh off, Church, you shitey bashtard!'

My friends and his started laughing and he just stood there in disbelief, the drool dripping from his gaping mouth. He looked at his mates creased up with laughter and all he could manage was, 'Eh?'

I pressed home my advantage. 'What you gonna do? Get your dad onto me?' (what he'd famously said to a sixth–former who had smacked him for bullying his little brother in the same year as me.)

One of Church's mates came over to say he thought my impersonation was really good and asked if I could do any of the teaching staff, as well. Before I could take any requests, Church was at the front of the queue and was being served. There was no immediate retaliation and, although I did get a good 'shoe-ing' later in the day, the bullying was never quite as bad again.

I soon discovered that another of the best ways to get accepted at the school and limit any bullying, was to get involved in sport. I was never good at any particular sport, but 'God loves a trier' and my trials appeared to be appreciated by other students and even sort of recognised by the perspicacious and eloquent PE department. My PE report at the end of Year 7 was the detailed and very helpful, 'A keen trier – diet?'

I started out in the first year playing rugby union, quickly discovering that whereas I had the stature to play at prop forward, I did not possess the lung capacity or stamina to make a valuable contribution for more than a few minutes at a time. I always felt that the scrum seemed to stay down for much longer than necessary, and when it eventually broke up, the ball was at least fifty metres away and it was time for us front-row forwards to trundle off to the next break-down in play. I also got injured in one match when the entire ruck/maul collapsed on top of me. I felt acute pain in the back of my neck and shoulder and it seemed to hurt to move my neck in any direction. The match continued on around me and it was only when the referee came to set the next scrum that he realised that the fattest prop was missing. He was actually trying to stand up at the other end of the pitch and was grimacing every time he tried to move. A cursory 'check-up from the neck up' performed by the ref was met with a shrug of the shoulders and another member of staff was dispatched to drive me down to the hospital in central Stockport. I was expecting the worst – probably paralysis and a lifetime confined to a wheelchair. The doctor, however, had other ideas and after twisting and contorting my arms, shoulders and neck for a few minutes, which was unbelievably painful, declared, with the aid of an interpreter, that I had not broken my neck. He wrote a letter to my doctor and told me to hand it over when I next saw him. The same night I visited my doctor and he shared its contents. It went something like:

Dear Doctor,

This eleven year old boy had hurt his neck whilst rolling over via the head. On examination his neck was not broken.

Regards,

A Quack

My doctor confirmed this diagnosis and gave me some pain killers, recommending that I rested my neck and shoulders from the scrum for a few weeks. As a result I got permission from the school to swap from rugby to the other option, lacrosse – which was deemed to be much safer.

To the uninitiated, lacrosse is legalised warfare. It is billed as the fastest game on two feet (not when I played it) and consists of eleven people on each side, armed with heavy sticks with a net at one end, chasing after a vulcanised rubber ball and being given the consent to barge, check and beat your opponents with your stick. The object of the game is to score a goal in a small net the size of a sentry box, but more importantly, survive without serious injury. It was recommended that you wore a helmet, gloves and shin pads, but they were purely optional. I got a second-hand stick, a new pair of gloves and the cheapest version of a helmet, made of cricket-pad-material with a detachable metal visor. It certainly only served to cushion the blow when you got 'checked' on the head. It was also recommended that you wore a special padded body protector (like the lead jacket they used to put on you when you had an X-ray at the dentist) and a box if you were 'in goal.'

On one occasion I was asked to play in goal (I suppose they thought I'd fill the goal and make it almost impossible for the opposition to score), but was not offered any of the aforementioned protection. I lasted about fifteen minutes until a vicious snap shot bounced off the turf and hit me straight in the 'meat and two veg.' I went down like a factory chimney, landing on the ball. I had to be revived and carried from the pitch, before the opposition were awarded a penalty, as the keeper hadn't released the ball in the required four seconds. I tell you – when you get hit by a lacrosse ball, you stay hit. They were rock hard and left massive bruising if ever you were unlucky enough to be hit by one.

The school had suffered a number of broken windows from errant lacrosse balls and there were strict rules banning their use in the playground or anywhere within twenty-five yards of any building. However, we felt that if you were extremely careful, you could get away with it. One lunchtime I was practicing underarm passes with my mate, H, on the tarmac at the back of school (a 'no ball games' area). We were just bouncing the ball along the hard surface so that it seemed to gather pace as it reached your partner. I sent along one fizzer that bounced over H's stick and then all of a sudden a shiny white car appeared from the side of the building. (Staff sometimes drove cars up to this area of the school to allow them to turn round, so that they were facing the right way for the journey home). It was the aforementioned geriatric French teacher who had nipped out at lunch time to collect his brand new shiny white Austin Maxi from the garage. He came to a halt to put the car in reverse to commence his turning manoeuvre, just as the speeding lacrosse ball thudded menacingly into his front near-side hubcap. H and I stood open-mouthed and motionless as the ancient teacher gave a startled look and peered left, right and back again. Fortunately we were too far away for him to see us and we quickly hid the lacrosse sticks behind a wall. We nonchalantly walked onto the school field as we saw the teacher lift the car's bonnet and appear to scratch his head in confusion. After a few minutes, he closed the bonnet, checked all along the off-side of the car and parked up. We retrieved the ball from a nearby flowerbed and walked in for afternoon school. At the end of the day, I walked past his car and there on the front near-side hubcap of this pristine car was a small round dent, remarkably similar in diameter to that of a lacrosse ball.

The other winter sport that was the bane of my life was the dreaded cross-country run. This usually started off with a 'warm-up jog' of a lap or two around the school playing field before leaving the grounds and pounding down the leafy drives of Davenport and through a housing estate before emerging on the main A6. As one of the 'fat wheezy boys', I possessed neither the speed nor stamina for this sport. I was always in the back two at the start and after a half-mile or so, was usually trailed off last. Usually, I would be running alongside one of the PE staff who would urge me to,

'Run through the pain. Keep it going. Think of Frank Shorter (the 1972 Olympic marathon winner) and run through the pain. Forget about the asthma attack, it's a sign of weakness!'

It's a sign of weakness alright – a sign of weak lungs and in those days, I had not been proscribed an inhaler to bring any relief. After about a mile, I would accept the inevitable defeat and with hands on hips would stop to take in great gasps of much-needed oxygen. The teacher would also realise he was fighting a losing battle and, as he sprinted off to find the next straggler, would turn and shout,

'You'll be alright. Walk back to school in your own time.'

I'd turn round and slowly drag myself back the way we'd come, sometimes arriving after the others had returned, showered and on some occasions even moved onto their next lesson or lunch.

In my first year at SGS, we also had swimming every Wednesday afternoon. This was a throwback to the old days of all boys having PE on this afternoon and attending Saturday morning school for normal lessons to pay back the missed academic time. Fortunately for me, Saturday schooling had been stopped the year I started, but the contract with Stockport Baths continued. As a result, every Wednesday lunch time the weak swimmers of the first year (not surprisingly I was in this group as a non-swimmer) would catch one of the regular 92 service buses down into Stockport for forty minutes of swimming. I'd had 'swimming lessons' at junior school where the instructor, Mrs Fag (so named because of the Park Drive constantly hanging from her lips) would simply shout,

'Non-swimmers in the shallow end and try to swim,' as she devoted her attention to the experienced swimmers and lighting up her next cigarette.

At Stockport Baths, I was shocked to discover that the instructor was a doppelganger for Mrs Fag. You could tell this place was more up-market though, because she would shout out,

'Non-swimmers in the shallow end and use them floats. Do as many widths as you can,' as she devoted her attention to the experienced swimmers and lighting up her next cigarette.

I told my fellow non-swimmers about Stalybridge Baths and Mrs Fag and we decided that her Stockport twin should be called 'Mrs Ash.'

The sports I enjoyed most at school were badminton, cricket and darts – yes I did say darts. I got to be quite good at badminton (if I say so myself) and on one occasion beat one of the cocky first XV rugby players, who reckoned he was the best at everything and challenged me to a game. He only did it the once. I also beat him in the 6th form darts competition, much to his dismay - I can remember him cheering loudly as I was eventually beaten in the final. Incidentally, darts was a 'big thing' in the sixth form at SGS. Stockport had been dubbed the 'World Capital of Darts' with legends such as Leighton Rees and Alan Evans regular visitors to, and players in, the town. Even today it is home to the darting royalty of Tony 'The Silverback' O'Shea and Darryl 'The Dazzler' Fitton. It was cricket though that I enjoyed the most.

I think it would be fair to describe my cricketing skills as somewhere between mediocre and abysmal. I batted (badly) left-handed, as I'd been taught that way by my left-handed dad. I bowled right handed and usually delivered a variety of slow wide balls or slow full tosses to make the batsman feel at home. My fielding was little better – I couldn't throw the ball that far and often was asked to field 'silly mid-on' or 'silly mid-off' to every bowler, pace or spin. Again, the captain probably felt that my large frame would block off the chance of a boundary on one side of the wicket. For once, I had the correct equipment. Cricket whites were part of the statutory school uniform and after the 'lacrosse accident', I had invested in my own box – for batting and close-in fielding. Batting pads and gloves were provided by the school when needed and there were even communal boxes, usually attached to a jock-strap. It became part of the initiation ceremony for new players that we convinced them to wear it outside their cricket clothes. This came to a stop however, when one poor lad was told that it was a new helmet and he was to tie the jockstrap under his chin. When he went out to bat, our opponents were rolling around in hysterics, but our umpire, a strict disciplinarian, didn't see the funny side of it and we were all reprimanded.

Cricket matches were either played on a Wednesday or Saturday afternoon, the former being the more popular as you got to miss half a day of lessons. Some of the squad refused to play on a Saturday and so I tended to get a chance to represent the school in some of these games. Whatever the result, you always looked forward to the tea interval for the splendid array of sandwiches and cakes – very civilised. If we played at home, tea would be served in our canteen and although the fare on offer always looked good, you had to make sure you knew who had made it, or should I say 'handled it.' I say this on account of an incident in the SGS canteen which has traumatised me ever since. . .

It has to be said that the food served at SGS was not as good as that on offer in Stalybridge. After a number of parental complaints, a new chef was brought in to oversee the dinner ladies and overhaul the service. He made quite an impression in his white chef's outfit, yet failed to bother to cover his unruly long ginger hair. He also sported a pair of thick-rimmed spectacles which magnified his pupils to an alarming degree. His culinary revolution meant that the 'new look' menu now included a range of new more appetising items, including chips and a custard/jam/coconut/pastry concoction which we were told was 'Manchester Tart'. Every time this dessert appeared, somebody would ask one of the dinner ladies,

'What's the dessert, please?'

'It's 'Manchester Tart."

This would bring about much sniggering and innuendo that the chef (whom we'd nicknamed 'Crusty' - like Rusty on account of his red hair, but slightly dirtier) liked his Manchester Tarts.

Anyway, back to the trauma. On one lunchtime in the middle of serving, all was going smoothly. Doris was serving two or three fish fingers on each plate, before handing it to Janice to apply a large pile of chips. She then passed the plate to Crusty who ladled on a serving from a large vat full of steaming baked beans. He asked each boy,

'Beans?'

When answered in the affirmative, Crusty seemed to turn up his nose as he peered through his steamed-up glasses into the metal bowl to discover the steaming mass of beans. And then disaster struck. The student before me said 'Yes' to the question and as Crusty scowled down at the offending beans, his spectacles slipped off his nose and landed in the bowl, quickly sinking in the sea of tomato sauce.

'Shit!' breathed Crusty and he plunged a hand into the bubbling beans to retrieve his glasses. He pulled out the specs and after uttering an almost inaudible 'F**k!' he wiped the steaming bean juice off his hand before licking the beans and tomato sauce from the now – steaming eyewear. Within seconds the glasses were back on his face and he turned to me,

'Beans?' he asked.

I stood open-mouthed at what I'd just witnessed, before pulling myself together and offering a cheery

'Not today, thanks.'

I couldn't believe it and the next few people in the queue who had witnessed the action for some reason all declined Crusty's offer of baked beans. People further back in the queue had no idea about what had happened and within a matter of minutes Crusty had managed to empty his bowl. It was for this reason that some of the cricketers appeared to be very interested in the food and who was handling it.

Apart from cricket matches, the most important sporting occasion was the annual Sports Day. Once again, this took part on a Saturday afternoon and attendance was compulsory. I got to represent my house, Nicholson, at the shot put. They thought that my big frame would bring good results, but they didn't realise that Arden House had a secret weapon in Norman Austin. Whilst the other competitors and I all threw within a couple of metres of each other, Norman was like Geoff Capes on acid. He wasn't big like Big Ian was big, but I've never seen anybody as strong. It is honestly true that his first throw sailed over the marked-out area and once it hit the deck, continued to roll through a privet hedge and into an adjoining property. The event had to be suspended until one of the helpers had been given permission by the Headmaster to run round to the house and ask the neighbour if he could collect the shot from the middle of his lawn. The event was awarded to Norman (he'd not just beaten the school record, he'd smashed it) and for his remaining throws he was given a heavier, adult shot, which even he was unable to throw off school property.

Straying off school property was a big no-no – hence the need to get permission from the head to reclaim the shot. There were various areas that were 'out of bounds' at different times of the day. The main drive, the junior school field, the corridors, the driveway to the Headmaster's House and the tennis courts were prime examples. I was even kicked off the tennis courts during a PE lesson once by the Headmaster, for wearing a yellow 'Fred Perry' tennis shirt – apparently, although it had passed the inspection of the PE department, it was a strict rule that whites had to be worn on certain courts. With no other PE kit in my bag, I returned to play wearing my normal school shirt, but without the tie and this was deemed to be perfectly acceptable.

On one side, the school was bordered by 'The Convent' Girls' School and this was the 'out of bounds' area that was guarded the most. Some of the sixth formers used to chat over the gate with their lady friends and it had been known for some lads to dig a hole through the hedge in an attempt to gain freedom and enter the Promised Land. It was also a hangout for the 'cool' smokers, who liked to share a ciggy with any willing female. As a result, staff would normally patrol the border at break times, although it was rumoured that at least one male member of the SGS staff was keen on one of the Convent staff and would occasionally appear at the gate with a pack of ten, just on the off chance. The far side of the playing field though was a much better hideout for smokers – you were at least a hundred metres from the school, you could drop down into the ditch next to the railway line and if a member of staff did appear, you had a good minute or so to scurry along the ditch to find a better hiding place. To be honest, the smokers here were largely ignored until one lad managed to set fire to a large portion of the banking whilst allegedly playing with a magnifying glass.

The school took fire really seriously and fire practices were common. On one occasion the alarm sounded in the middle of a German lesson with one of my favourite teachers of all time and the nicest man you could meet, Mr Herman. This guy was a legend. I think his name was 'Wolfgang' Herman, but to everybody at SGS, he was 'Mr Herman' (to his face) or 'Willie' (behind his back). He spoke in a thick German accent and was a maverick wrapped up in an enigma. He didn't need any fancy wall displays or computers to bring the subject to life - he had his trusty tape recorder and his home-made buzzer, which he pressed to let out a frightening retort every time a boy made a mis-pronunciation of a German word.

On one occasion, we got to class early and one student managed to break into his desk and detach the buzzer from its massive battery supply. As soon as Willie arrived, we waited in anticipation for him to get the buzzer out to start correcting us. After what seemed like an age, he reached into his desk drawer and placed the buzzer in front of him. He asked one of the students to start reading from a page in the text book and the lad started to a make some terrible deliberate mistakes. Willie pressed the buzzer, but to no avail. He pressed again and again. He uttered a few 'Was ist..?' and at least a couple of 'Scheisse's' before bellowing, 'Nein! Nein! Es ist kaput!' He brought the lesson to a halt, set us some written work and got out a screwdriver to repair the damage he didn't know that we'd inflicted.

Our favourite mis-pronunciation, which we were always on the lookout for, was the German word for 'newspaper', which is 'Zeitung.' The German 'Z' is pronounced like a 'TS' and heaven help anyone who got this wrong. Willie would press his buzzer and interrupt the offender with a,

'Nein! It's not 'Seitung', it's 'Tseitung!' Say 'Tseitung, Tseitung!"

'Seitung, Seitung'

The buzzer would sound again.

'Nein!! Say 'Raats, Raats'

'Raats, Raats'

'Ts, Ts'

'Ts, Ts'

'Ja, now say 'Zeitung!"

'Seitung!'

The buzzer would be held down to mask the 'Nein!!!!!' and some other German expletives and deletives and the whole process would either start again from the beginning or end in a resigned abject failure.

Anyway, back to the fire alarm. On this particular day, it was a simple walk-through to allow new students and staff to familiarise themselves with the routine. Everybody had been informed in advance, or so we thought. We were sitting in our German lesson on the top floor of the old school when the alarm rang. We all stood up and remained in silence behind our desks to await instructions, as per the school rules. We looked towards Mr Herman and saw a wave of panic take him over,

'Oh my God! There's a fire. Quick, what do we do?'

'Run for our lives?' suggested one helpful student.

'Oh my God! What about all my new text books?' yelled Mr H, as he quickly retrieved his buzzer from the desk.

'Throw them out of the window?' another boy chipped in.

'Ja. That is a good idea. Quick – all the books out of the window. Now!'

The boys were only too happy to fling piles of textbooks, new and old, exercise books and piles of loose papers all out of the second floor window on to the heads of the unsuspecting students, walking briskly and orderly for the field and their designated emergency registration areas. They looked up in amazement and started to run to avoid the falling debris.

Another student asked, 'Do you want me to throw out your tape recorder and boxes of tapes from the cupboard?'

'No. There is no time. All of you – out now – save yourselves!'

We ran down the stairs, some of us failing to restrain our urge to break into laughter. After being registered by our form teacher, we returned to Mr Herman's room to see what would happen next. We didn't have long to wait before a red-faced Mr Herman appeared. He entered, shaking his head in disbelief, but he had a slight grin on his face as he said,

'5A - you absolute bastards!'

We spent the rest of the lesson retrieving the equipment and putting his room back to normal. Willie was one of those inspirational teachers who you'll always remember for who he was, rather than what he did. He reminds us all of the essential central role of the teacher. Teaching is changing all the time and teachers are now often assessed by the content of their planning folder or the quality of their student exercise books and marking, rather than what's going on in the classroom – but it IS this that is the most important. It's who you are and how you interact with the students that is of paramount importance. It was through teachers like Willie that I started to realise that 'Banter for Learning', as Hywel Roberts calls it, is the secret to being a successful teacher and it was something I quite fancied trying.

Another great teacher was the ancient Deputy Head, 'Bill', who was brought in to teach us English Literature in our GCE year. He was always smartly dressed in his suit and teacher's robes and was a real eccentric. He always insisted on tidiness and instructed boys to place their briefcases (another compulsory item at SGS) under their chairs and never, ever in the aisles. When he arrived for the lesson, all the boys would stand up behind their desks as Bill swept in; he looked everybody up and down and walked up and down the aisles, booting any errant briefcase with terrific force – it was rumoured that he was a fearsome rugby player in his youth and I bet he was a kicker. Obviously every lesson some students deliberately left bags in the aisles to create the fun. Bill had a really dry sense of humour and although many of his lessons could seem dull, students were always on the lookout for the next piece of humour. When reading sections from set books or poems, Bill would always start with,

'And who should we have to read now?'

He would pretend to consult his register, before announcing with a twinkle in his eye,

'Ah, yes. It's time for Torkington to read!'

Torkington (one of my best mates) would read every lesson and sometimes would read two or three times in succession, each time preceded with the 'And who should we have to read now?' Some students believed this was because Torkington was the only name Bill could remember – after all, he had taught three of the Torkington brothers before the one in my year. In truth though, you could tell from the smile on his lips and in his eyes that Bill knew exactly what he was doing and was in on the joke.

Bill also liked to have fun with any visitor to the classroom, who would leave bemused, amused or even slightly abused. One regular visitor to the classroom would be the duty prefect who would visit each classroom to ask for any absentees and Bill was in his element. He was happy to play to the crowd and it would usually go something like,

'Excuse me, Sir. Have you got any absentees?'

'I don't know. They're not here. Now let me see .....Guthlac.........Wiglaf....... Hrothgar.....You're not writing any of these down.'

'Sorry, Sir. I'll do that now.'

'Make sure you spell 'Hrothgar' correctly.'

And then he would read out the real absentees.

Not all staff were as funny or inspirational as Bill or Willie. I can remember Geography teachers being particularly sleep-inducing. One of them was a stickler for detail and wanted accuracy and neatness above all else. I can remember one homework task he set to use an Ordnance Survey map to calculate the distances by train from Stockport Edgeley to ten different railway stations. This involved a complicated method of marking a piece of paper and bending it around the black lines on the map. The teacher insisted on accuracy to within one – tenth of a mile – almost impossible to cack-handed first years, but not you would think to an avid train spotter who had relatives who drove trains for British Rail and access to their manuals. He calmly recorded all the official figures and awaited the inevitable 10/10. He was awarded 2/10 and when he questioned some of the teacher's figures, he was told that there was no possibility of the teacher being incorrect – that's Geography for you.

Biology was similarly bland until we were subjected to a new teacher who thought he was trendy. He had been known to wear a cravat and didn't realise that nobody was as impressed with him as he was himself. In our first lesson, he greeted us with,

'Hi! I'm Mr Walker and I'm not your regular type of Biology teacher.' (He probably meant he didn't have the leather patches on his jacket, suffer from third-degree halitosis and had no intention of planning any lessons).

He informed us that he would start by asking some 'general questions' to assess our level of competence and understanding. His first question was the only one I recall –

'Why do we have a penis? Hammond?'

Poor old Hammy didn't see that one coming. He shuffled nervously on his stool before stuttering an answer,

'Er....it's a......well, it's....... it's peculiar to the species.'

'Yours may be Hammond, but mine certainly isn't!'

Boom! There you have it. How to be an arrogant Biology teacher without even trying. His replacement fared even worse. She (it was a bit of a novelty to see a female teacher at an all-boys school) made the mistake in one of her first lessons of holding up a drawing of the 'male reproductive organ' and asking the question, 'Has everybody got one of these?' Cue a couple of students starting to rummage down their trousers to check.

I actually managed to escape with a grade 'B' at GCE Biology, much to the annoyance of the Science staff who were convinced I would fail – after all, I got a mere 9% in the mock. I remember going through the actual paper after the exam with the teacher and some other students. The others were puzzled by a graph question and when I told them my answer, based on logic, the teacher said that it was worth 4/4, but put me down at the same time by saying,

'Of course, it's not really a proper Science question. You often find some of the weaker candidates pick up marks here!'

I was also one of the 'weaker candidates' when it came to practical subjects. I can remember being given last place in Art in every assessment or report. I hadn't the skill or patience to produce anything at all reasonable. My favourite Art lesson was when we did 'potato prints' and this was only because the teacher made us save half of our potatoes so that he could fry them in a chip pan on his portable gas stove on the art room floor. We only ever got two or three chips each, but the smell was amazing. Can you imagine Health and Safety regulations allowing this today?

Woodwork was another crazy lesson. We were taught how to make all the different joints and once we had mastered this, we were allowed to make what we wanted. Boys were making cabinets and coffee tables whilst I struggled to make a table tennis bat and a box with a sliding lid for snooker balls. We were taught by a guy who was at least 108 and regularly had coughing fits (wood dust or his 60 a day smoking habit – take your pick) which we frequently thought would be his last. He also had a massive temper and would either whack you on the head with your faulty piece of woodwork or throw it, a mallet or a chisel at you with some force.

Such violence was accepted by students at a time when corporal punishment in school still existed. Punishment at SGS usually took the form of detention or lines, but the cane was still part of the arsenal. I can remember getting my first lines in December of my first year, shortly after we'd moved house and when power cuts were a regular occurrence. I struggled by candlelight to copy out 50 times, 'I must not disturb Mr Mathieson during his teaching of Shakespeare to the Lower Literary Fifth.' Apparently the whole form were noisy in the corridor whilst waiting for our next lesson, so all 30 boys were given lines and Mr Mathieson was able to feed the bin with 1,500 versions of his rubric.

Detentions could be given by staff or prefects. Staff tended to give you detentions in multiples of thirty minutes. It was quite common for a member of staff to say, 'Take three 30 minute detentions.' This meant that you had to stay after school on three separate occasions with that member of staff to do your time. Some staff were prepared to do two in one go and you knew that certain staff never gave detentions, because they couldn't be bothered to stay after school. Prefect detentions were different again. The prefects had their own 'special room' just off the quad with a kettle, fridge, toaster and a black-and-white television without an aerial. You might get to spend the time in there, although if there were a few miscreants, a prefect would take the detention in a classroom instead. Some prefects were power-crazed and would issue 'three thirty minuters' for smiling in the corridor, or 'looking at them funny'. Most were reasonable and would often let you go early from a detention so that they could get back to their toast and telly.

Corporal punishment was rarely used. Boys knew that the Deputy Head, even though he was a lovely old man and a caring teacher, had the reputation of being a savage caner. The Head, on the other hand, allegedly couldn't knock the skin off a rice pudding. On one occasion in my second year I was playing football in the school yard after school one night. One of the lads hoofed the ball over the 'goal' and onto the roof of the one-storey building at one end of the playground. He expertly shinned up a drainpipe and hauled himself up onto the roof. At that precise moment, the Headmaster, dressed as usual in his three-piece suit and full academic robes, appeared at the top of the steps into the yard. We all froze, but then as the Head descended into the yard, he was startled by a football seemingly appearing from nowhere. He turned and spotted our friend on the apex of the roof.

'What do you think you are doing up there? Come down here immediately!'

The footballer retraced his steps and walked quickly to the Headmaster.

'Sorry, sir. Just retrieving the ball for the lads.'

'Boys are not allowed on the roof of the school. It is out of bounds and extremely dangerous. Take three thirty minute detentions or three strikes of the cane.'

'Who's doing the caning, sir?'

'Me. Why?'

'I'll take the caning then.'

'Present yourself to my office at 10a.m. tomorrow.'

The next day the caning took place, as arranged, and our friend reported that he had 'felt nowt.'

Not all mis-deeds received punishment or even got noticed. One of my favourites involved a Maths teacher who we felt never really paid attention. On one hot summer's day, he was teaching our class on the ground floor of the main building and all the old metal windows had been flung wide open. Right at the back of the class, one boy noiselessly climbed out of the window, dropping down into the yard below. The teacher was busy writing up copious questions on the board and noticed nothing. The lad quickly ran back into the building and within a minute was knocking on the classroom door. The teacher barely looked up from the board and shouted,

'Enter.'

'Sorry I'm late, sir.'

'That's fine. Take a seat.'

The boy grinned and gave us the thumbs up. We struggled to contain our laughter, but somehow we successfully passed a message back to the lad,

'Dares you to do it again!'

Without a word he dived out the window again, before re-appearing at the door a minute later. After knocking on the door once more and being asked to 'enter', the lad continued with,

'Sorry I'm late, sir.'

The teacher's brow furrowed – perhaps he sensed 'déjà vu?'– but once more he retorted with,

'That's fine. Take a seat.'

The class went wild. The teacher shouted for us to concentrate on the twenty simultaneous equations he was writing on the board and the boy passed into legendary status, well, at least for a few weeks. (Actually it was rumoured that in another class he sat at the back by some full length blackout curtains and successfully removed every stitch of clothing and took a bow, quickly re-dressing before the end of the lesson)

In spite of all this, Mathematics was one of the subjects I'd always enjoyed (after all I was the Heather Grinter Mathematics Prize Winner at St Paul's in 1971), but at first it became a grind at SGS. In those pre-calculator and pre-computer days, it was all textbooks, problems and trying to fathom out how to use a slide rule. My first experience of a computer was one that had been built by a group of geeks from the school with the help of some equally –nerdy Science and Maths teachers. It was housed in the cavernous basement of the Junior School at SGS and was full of electrical cabinets and whirling tapes, like on some bad 1950's Sci-Fi set. The spotty geek who gave us a tour of the beast, was immensely proud of this hardware but as far as I could tell, it served no purpose whatsoever - it just made a lot of weird whirring noises and seemed to use up a lot of electricity. I couldn't envisage it ever catching on. You'd have to have some sort of mansion to be able to house a 'home computer' in those times. At my final 'Annual Prize-Giving and Speech Night' in 1978, all students were given a small piece of card with what looked like a piece of grit taped onto it. The main speech-giver and guest of honour from Manchester University told us that it was something called a 'microchip' and that it would revolutionise the world. As I walked on stage to collect the 'Lord Vernon Latin Prize', I remember thinking as I shook the guy's hand, 'You're as mad as a box of frogs, aren't you? I've got fillings bigger than your microchip. By the look of your jacket, you'd be better off trying to invent a decent dandruff shampoo to revolutionise your world.'

Calculators too didn't appear until the mid-1970's and I remember paying £30 for a state of the art (it had a percentage key) Rockwell calculator, which I was allowed to use at home, but not at school. Again, I wasn't too impressed. It was too expensive, you had to change the batteries every few weeks and for most sums it was quicker to use your brain. Most of my mates got more kicks from turning the display screen for '7100553, 71077345 and above all, 58008' upside down to reveal 'Esso Oil, Shell Oil and Boobs.'

At the start of my third year, the school discovered the new 'Modern Maths' syllabus and three years of Venn diagrams and the like were delivered by an enthusiastic P.E. teacher, roped in for the job, in about six weeks. Algebra, Trigonometry and Geometry were made so much simpler and by the end of Year 11, twenty-eight out of the thirty lads in my class had achieved a Grade 'A' in Maths and although we continued to use log tables instead of calculators, the slide rule had been assigned to the scrap heap of obsolete technology.

Out of all the lessons, it was completely obvious that History lessons were the best. Well, as a History teacher, it was inevitable that I would say that. I had the pleasure to be taught by three of the very best - Mr Coulson, Dr Holmes and above all, the recently departed Mr Henshall, or 'Nick the Fruit', as the boys called him. They were all good story tellers and made History come alive for me. I would take inordinate care with my History homework and, in the days before the Internet, became a regular sight in local libraries doing research. In the first year, we had to write biographies for up to twenty people from Tudor times and I spent all my pocket money on Jackdaw folders which contained excellent sources and resources for the task. In the third year, I took it a stage further by spending half of my life at Stockport Library, making use of their copious resources on the 'Cotton Industry in the Industrial Revolution' – I became so obsessed that I even opted to explain the workings of Hargreaves' 'Spinning Jenny' in my GCE French oral exam.

You could always share a laugh and a joke in History lessons, but History was always hard work. Homework tasks were given weekly – you might have to answer questions from sources, write an account of the information delivered in the lesson or even produce a presentation or prepare to speak in a debate. If this was the case, Nick would usually shine the light from his overhead projector into your face, so that it seemed you were being interrogated. In double lessons, he used to allow us a two-minute break to move around and re-settle and once hinted that he wished he had time to nip out for a coffee. The next lesson, much to his amusement, I turned up with a flask, and the coffee break became a feature of all future double lessons. We didn't always see eye to eye – my placement in the lower set for A Level History after attaining a Grade A at GCE still rankles today – but my future career and love of History owes a lot to him and the History Department at SGS.

My last visit to the school came a few months after I left. I was persuaded to attend an Old Stopfordians dinner at the school by three other friends, who were also ex-students who I had gone Inter-Railing with in Italy and France. This reminded me once again of how I wasn't your archetypal Old Stopfordian. In my hired dinner suit, I watched in some amusement as, during the after-dinner speeches, grown men shouted, 'Shame!' and booed the announcement that from the next year, the school was to open its doors for the very first time to girls. This was one of the last times I saw these three friends together in one place – all three went to Cambridge; one went on to become a managing director of a multi-national company, one has a very responsible job in the Palace of Westminster and the other, a high-ranking lawyer, became the Chairman of Governors at SGS. I went to Leeds and became a History teacher.

God's Own County

If I sometimes felt like a fish out of water at SGS, my move to Leeds in God's Own County was like coming home. Perhaps the ancient French teacher with his 'All stations east of Stalybridge' gibe was trying to tell me something. There was something about the university, the city and the people that made me feel at ease – it was almost as if I'd found my place.

I was accepted as a student for the BA in History course and prepared to move away from home for the first time. I was looking forward to expanding my historical education, but what I really needed was education in life. Apart from my month's 'Inter-railing' around France and Italy, I had never been away from home for more than a week but my move across the Pennines proved to be a permanent one.

For my first year, like the majority of students, I'd opted to accept the university's offer of accommodation. I'd hoped for a hall of residence with most meals provided, but instead was given a single room on the top floor of a large male-only, university-owned Victorian house, with self-catering the only option. It was built right next door to the old Leeds Maternity Hospital. Little was I to know that a good night's sleep was to become a rarity, especially in the warmer months when the hospital had its old sash windows opened to the max. I learnt more swear words from the shouts and screams of the women in the labour ward than I had in my previous 18 years on this earth.

My room was the smallest of about six bedrooms on the cavernous top floor (possibly the original servants' quarters) and contained a small single bed, a desk and chair and a wardrobe – you had to push the chair right under the desk to be able to be able to open the wardrobe door slightly. There was a shower room and about two toilets and sinks for all of the top floor residents to share, but there was no other communal space on the floor. In fact, the only communal area was three floors down in the basement, where the kitchen contained a number of ancient free-standing gas cookers, three or four filthy fridges and a large central table that could seat about sixteen people. It was here that all the male residents, representatives from all over the world and with widely varying culinary skills, descended to cook their meals in the early evening.

The strangest resident was a guy from Sudan. He was well over six feet in height and sported a mass of dark curly hair and beard, which contrasted greatly from the pristine white gowns he always wore. He seemed to have a never-ending string of girlfriends of all nationalities who used to block the communal telephone (housed in an enclosed booth next to the kitchen – remember these were the days before mobile phones) with their calls. They were always trying to get hold of him and some would appear at all hours of the day or night to lay siege to the house. The guy himself was very quiet and unassuming. He would glide into the kitchen and start to make a variety of strange –looking foodstuffs. When the food was deemed to be ready, he would then serve up from the pans and bowls directly onto the bare Formica communal table. The other residents would gaze on in a mixture of shock and disgust as three or four large dollops of hot and cold food appeared on the table, before being mopped up by the chef (and occasionally one of the chosen ones from his harem) with a handful of what looked like pancakes or chapatis.

Meal times were always entertaining and people were curious to see what strange creations could be found that were so alien to their own culture and experience. One lad usually seemed to be cooking reeking pans of liver, kidneys or heart (always to be found cheap at Leeds City Market) and the vegetarians tended to sit at as far away as possible from him at meal times. Another's favourite dessert was a large bowlful of vanilla ice cream sprinkled with a bag of salted peanuts and topped off with a can of coke. Apparently, these were his three favourite things and he didn't think he should be denied the ultimate pleasure of having all three together. The worst though was when a couple of lads caught Zhang Wei, a Chinese student, eating a can of Pedigree Chum dogfood. They looked on in horror as he shovelled a few large spoonfuls straight from the can down his throat, before intervening and explaining that Chum was intended only for canine consumption. The poor lad didn't speak very good English, but he was able to convey that he had seen a picture of a dog on the side of the tin and had jumped to the conclusion that it was tinned dog. Apparently, dog was a real treat in his part of China, where children were given a puppy as a present. They would play with the puppy until the day came when it was ready to be slaughtered and eaten.

One of the strangest chefs in the residence was Jez. One of his favourite dishes was a ham hock cooked in a large vat of mushy peas, which used to stink the kitchen out. On one occasion he was rushed into hospital – it was rumoured with food-poisoning. When one of his mates went to visit, he was asked to throw away the remains from Jez's ham and pea concoction, which he'd left on a stove. On returning to the house, the pan could not be found. When Jez got back a week later, the pan was re-discovered, overflowing with mould, at the back of the larder. Apparently some other resident had cleared it away from the cooker and thought Jez might want it on his return. In the second year, I shared a house with Jez and I'm sorry to say his cooking habits did not improve. He was always really hungry and even started to resent the time wasted on cooking food and serving it on plates. Accordingly, he graduated from eating shredded pineapple and evaporated milk straight from the can to doing the same for uncooked Campbell's meatballs and Heinz Big Soup – please don't try this at home.

Sunday trading laws at the time meant that most shops were closed on the Sabbath and students who hadn't planned ahead could go hungry. Also many halls of residence often did not serve food on Sundays. This niche in the market was spotted by a very enterprising student. He happened to be in Leeds City Market late one Saturday afternoon when the traders were trying to close up. He saw that the butchers were offering terrific discounts on a vast array of meats to get rid of them and it gave him an idea. He bought up some packs of chops and steak and headed home. On Sunday morning, as hungover students raised themselves from their pits, he cycled round to a nearby hall of residence and offered his wares. He sold out in a matter of minutes, making a very healthy profit. The next week, he bought a much wider selection and made a much bigger profit and a regular Sunday business was born.

Other residents in my first student housing included a couple of guys from Guyana who were always good fun. Marlon was the 'house representative' who also ran our five-a-side football team and his mate, Bob, was one of the coolest and laid –back guys I've ever met. On one occasion they had a group of fellow Guyanans over to rehearse some reggae music they were performing at the annual 'International Festival' at the university. They sounded really good, but needed a catchy name for their newly-formed group. One lad suggested, 'Bob, Marlon and the W**kers', but I'm not sure they used it.

Apart from the kitchen, the main communal area for the residents was the pub - 'The Faversham', a three minute walk away or the Union Building, about another ten minutes further on. When I first started at Leeds, beer prices were low – you could get a pint of bitter for 25p or lager for 30p in the Union Bar – and not surprisingly, the bars were usually busy every night of the week. Three pints of bitter and three packets of crisps would set you back 99p – so you still had change from your one pound note.

The Union was a lifeline for many students. Apart from the low–priced bars, there were also a number of telephones with very small queues. If you lived off-campus, it would be a common sight to see a group of six or more students queuing outside a phone–box to make their weekly call home. You'd be armed with a few two-pence pieces (or ten-pence ones, if you wanted to have a long conversation and risk the wrath of the queue) and would make your one phone call. The Union also had three television rooms, one for each of the channels – BBC 1, BBC 2 and ITV. The ITV room would be busy for Coronation Street, but top attendance was in the small BBC 2 room for repeats of Monty Python, when literally hundreds of students swamped the area. It was always standing room only and people were known to stand huddled together on coffee tables at the back of the room, just to sneak a peek at the small television mounted on the wall. This was a time when television ownership amongst students was very low – in my third year, five of us clubbed together to pay Radio Rentals 50p per week to rent a tiny black-and-white set.

The Union also boasted a launderette (always busy), shower rooms, a bank, a small supermarket, a stationary shop, a record shop and upstairs, a snooker room. You could live in this building and by the look of some students, many did. At night it hosted discos, plays, comedy and bands – there was always something on. It was always well-run and there was never a hint of any trouble, even when big gigs and events were being staged. Local bands would play most nights and newly-formed student bands, including 'Bob, Marlon and the W**kers', often got their first gigs here.

One of my fellow house mates formed a punk band and they were given a slot in a 'local bands night'. They had rehearsed in a friend's house and had perfected three songs, which they were eager to perform. After a problem with the sound system and the first two bands over-running, they were told, 'one song only'. My mate seethed at the injustice of it all and after performing a very angry version of their self-penned 'No Compromise' to a less than appreciative audience, he finished with,

'I'd like to thank you all for being a great audience, but you haven't been. I think you're a shower of bastards and you can all f**k off!'

There was certainly 'no compromise' there. It could have 'all kicked off', but most people just cheered or nipped out to get another pint before the next act. Suffice it to say that they never performed at the university again and actually split up a few weeks later.

My next-door neighbour in the student flat was also a guitarist in a local group who were much more successful for a while, playing a few times in the Union, one time even supporting the headline act, Magazine, in the main hall. He studied 'Engineering' and as a result had 9 o'clock lectures every morning. At 6.30 a.m. every weekday without fail, I could hear through the paper-thin walls, the buzzer of his alarm clock , followed by him jumping out of bed and putting the single of 'Roxanne' by The Police on his record player. It would play at some volume as he shuffled across the landing, switched on the booming extractor fan in the shower room and added to the cacophony of sound with his rendition of, 'I wake up in the morning. What a pleasure it is!' I've never known what song this was from – maybe it was one of his group's self-penned tunes - but even today, nearly forty years later, I still find myself singing this as I enter the shower cubicle.

Unlike Engineering, the History Department at Leeds was very civilised. There were no nine o'clock lectures and even with the requirements of a subsidiary subject and language practice, my timetable only had about twelve hours of contact time and I finished for the weekend by midday Thursday. This allowed me plenty of time to do research in the library, play football and relax in the bar. Wednesday afternoons were also left free for sport and I often played five-a-side football with other members of my house or the History department. There were also football leagues and tournaments at different times, but the teams I tended to play for, 'The Elitists', 'Scunts' (the house team, named after a Guyanan swear word, according to Marlon) and the wonderfully-titled 'Oh Yes!', never really set the footballing world on fire.

'Oh Yes!' was named after a dodgy cheap 'chocolate-flavoured' bar you could get from a vending machine in the Union. The captain thought it'd be a good idea to run onto the pitch brandishing an 'Oh Yes!' bar, shake the hand of an opponent and offer them the chocolate, like exchanging pennants before a big game. It was also good when you turned up for a game with a team new to the league. They'd say,

'Excuse me; are you 'Oh Yes!'?

'OH YES!' we'd reply.

On one occasion we somehow made it through to the final day group stages of the annual university five-a-side tournament. We were drawn in a tough group against a team of West Indians who hit the ball harder than I'd ever seen, a team of scientists who'd given us a right hammering in the league and part of the university first XI, who were regarded as the pre-tournament favourites. After losing (badly) to the West Indians, but somehow beating the scientists, we faced the favourites in a must-win game. We'd noticed that they had been very cocky in their first two matches and thought they were better than everybody else. The tall blond striker was particularly loathsome. One of the 'Oh Yes!' guys, Paul, was a bit of a wind-up merchant and targeted Blondie for some abuse. The rules stated that for a deliberate foul anywhere on the pitch, the referee should award a penalty and send a player off. As soon as we were on the pitch, Paul taunted Blondie with,

'You think you're a right blond beauty, don't you?'

'Did you get your nails done when you went for that perm?'

'You look like a right nonce!'

That was the last straw. Blondie cracked. The next time Paul passed him, he was scythed down with a dreadful two-footed challenge, which could have landed Paul in hospital. The referee awarded a penalty, which Paul scored after winking at Blondie, but for some reason Blondie was not sent off (possibly because the referee happened to be the coach of the university team). This put us ahead against the favourites and for a few minutes a shock was on the cards, but the superior skill of our opponents soon shone through and they won with the last kick of the game.

At the end of my first year, all of the house residents applied for a further year in the house, but nobody was accepted. This resulted in a mad scramble over the summer holidays to find suitable student accommodation for the re-start in September. I joined forces with three other lads and our search began. In those days the choice of student housing was pretty down market. The house-hunting was left to Jez and I and the other two lads (Mark and Julian), who had gone home for the summer, agreed to abide with our choice. I must say we saw some absolute wrecks of houses and even a number of dodgy bed-sits in Roundhay without any windows, a hot plate shoved on the floor in the corner of the room and a shared toilet on a different floor. We were getting desperate and even looked at some areas which were not often used by students, including Hunslet and Bramley. We settled though on a four bedroomed mid-terrace on Tempest Road in Beeston in South Leeds, which would cost each of us the princely sum of £8 per week.

Beeston was four miles from Leeds, but on a regular bus route to the university. Tempest Road was a little run down, but we thought it would be fine and hoped it would meet the expectations of the others. Years later when holidaying in America, I turned on the television news to witness a story about rioting, looting and urban decay in Leeds. The pictures showed fighting in Beeston and the caption said, 'Tempest Road, Leeds – inner city squalor.' I also discovered later that Tempest Road was the boyhood home of one of my heroes, the Leeds poet, Tony Harrison. He also attended Leeds Grammar School, which also happens to be where I completed my teacher training – it's a small world. If I'd known this at the time, I'd have considered it to be fate and would have had no worries whatsoever about signing on the dotted line.

After heading into the centre of Leeds to complete the necessary paperwork and contacting the other lads from a public phone box to tell them the good news, we looked around for somewhere to have a celebratory lunch. We were standing outside the Merrion Centre and caught sight of a sign advertising 'The Hofbrauhaus', a German beer cellar, which promised lunch time food and entertainment. We descended the stairs to the cavernous cellar (once described by Alexei Sayle as reminiscent of the venue for Martin Bormann's stag night) and were stopped at the entrance booth and asked to purchase the required entrance ticket – 11p per person (10p plus VAT). As we entered the vast room of long tables and benches, we noticed that there were only about ten other patrons, including a couple with two children aged about seven and ten. We got a drink from the bar, ordered some food and sat down at one of the empty tables. Our conversation about our new house was interrupted by feedback from the PA system, followed by something like,

'Good afternoon, ladies and gentlemen and welcome to the Hofbrauhaus, home of the best in live entertainment. We're going to start proceedings with some dancing from our favourite go-go girl. Please welcome to the stage, Tina.'

A small splatter of applause and a few cheers from the family group (obviously related) welcomed the aforementioned Tina onto the stage. Patrick Hernandez launched into 'Born to be alive' and a small, thin and about 20-ish Tina started to gyrate. She was wearing a blue sparkly boob tube and matching mini skirt and was really getting into the music. I was quite impressed, but nearly choked on my recently arrived 'Hofbrauburger' when she removed the boob tube altogether! I glanced across to the family and they were just clapping and moving along to the music, as if there was nothing out of the ordinary. Worse was to follow. After the first number, there was no 'performance' for about ten minutes and then a new 'girl' was introduced. This 'girl' was 45, if she was a day, and her routine involved her removing all of her clothes – I still break into a cold sweat when I recall the varicose veins on her legs, reminiscent of a relief map of part of the Lake District. Suffice it to say – in the words of the News of the World, 'we made our excuses and left.' I did return to the venue on one more occasion shortly after we'd moved to

Tempest Road, to a 'Comic Strip' gig and witnessed Alexei Sayle introduce four up-and-coming young comedians – Rik Mayall, Adrian Edmondson, Dawn French and Jennifer Saunders. I wonder if they ever made it big?

When my parents first dropped me off at Tempest Road, they were shocked at how dirty the living areas and particularly the kitchen were. My mum had come armed with all manner of cleaning products and we set about removing the top layers of grime. We struggled at first, as the hot water supply didn't appear to be working, but after boiling up a few kettles, things got easier. Surprisingly, my bedroom – a very large attic room – was much cleaner and passed even my mum's eagle eye. After my parents left, the other lads started to arrive and I helped them move in. One of the more disturbing things we uncovered was a sort of 'poison pen' letter on the top of one of the wardrobes. It had been compiled from using cut-out letters from magazines and warned the previous Pakistani residents, and actual owners of the property, to leave Leeds or face the consequences.

The main problem with the house turned out to be the lack of any hot water, caused by a broken gas boiler. All rooms had individual gas fires, so keeping warm was not a problem, but the prospect of no hot water or baths was a serious concern. We contacted the letting agents in Leeds and they arranged for the gas board to inspect the boiler. They produced a report which said that the boiler could be taken away, repaired and re-instated for a cost of about £195. Alternatively, they could supply and fit a brand new boiler within a few days, for about £200. It seemed to us to be a no-brainer, but the owners took two weeks to reach a decision, eventually opting for the cheaper option. In the meantime we waited and waited as the days ticked by without any hot water. After a further four weeks of phone calls and letters to the agent, who blamed the delay on the gas board waiting for the required parts to fix the boiler, and surviving on the occasional shower at the university, we decided to take direct action.

Early one Saturday morning, all four of us caught a bus into Leeds, armed with soap, shampoo and towels. We headed for the agents office, located in York Place, a few streets away from the iconic international pool. The agents were trying to wrap up a tenancy agreement with a young couple as we entered the offices chanting, 'All we are saying is 'Give us a bath'!' We explained to the couple that as soon as you'd signed up with the agency, they didn't want to know. The manager was summoned and after listening to our grievances, he promised us an immediate rent reduction of 50% until the problem was sorted to our satisfaction and a cash pay-out to persuade us to leave and allow us to get a hot bath from the international pool and him to complete a deal with his prospective new tenants.

We walked in triumph around the corner to the pool (now sadly demolished) to be met by literally hundreds of people – mainly children – queuing up to enter the building. We went straight to the front and were confronted by a burly security guard who informed us that the pool was closed for an international gala and if we wanted to spectate, we'd have to join the queue. I explained that we had just come for a hot bath and we were shepherded in through a side door, much to the surprise and annoyance of the queuing masses. I think the hot bath was about 30p and it was housed in the basement.

There were a large number of separate cubicles, each with its own large metal bath and the four of us were given a numbered key for our bathroom. Even though we knew that people said that the facilities were only used by down-and-outs, it was really great to feel reasonably clean again.

Whilst we were down in that area, we stumbled across a trendy new wine bar, probably aimed mainly at the high-spending solicitors and lawyers whose offices littered the quarter. As we were now only paying £4 a week rent, we decided to give it a try. As we entered, we were asked to take a seat and a waitress would come to take our order. This was mighty strange for a group of (albeit very clean) students from Beeston. A young girl appeared and addressed Jez first of all,

'Good afternoon, sir. What can I get you?'

'A bitter, please.'

'I'm sorry, sir. We only serve lager.'

'A pint of lager, please.'

'I'm sorry, sir. We only serve halves.'

'Two halves of lager, please!'

After a quick drink of a number of halves, at a price more than four times our usual, we retired to the Union to continue our celebrations.

The reduced rent lasted for another four weeks until the re-conditioned boiler was finally ready. The gas board fitted it one afternoon and the early tests showed that the water was indeed hot. Jez was given the privilege of having the first bath – we thought he needed it the most. He took a canister of powdered Vim into the bathroom with him. We presumed it was to clean the bath afterwards, but he later reported that he had felt the need to use it as a scouring agent under his armpits. Unfortunately it also resulted in a distinctive red rash.

Living out in Beeston meant that you were a bit excluded from the socialising on campus and to compensate, we became regulars at our local pub, The Broadway on Dewsbury Road. We had an agreement that everybody finished university work by 9.30pm on a week-night and we'd then walk down for 'last orders.' (In those days, closing time was 10.30pm from Sunday to Thursday and 11pm on Friday and Saturday). Every night at closing time, Jez would declare that he was 'starving' and nine times out of ten we'd return home via the Chinese takeaway on Sunbeam Terrace, where, without fail, he would order chicken foo yung with boiled rice and try not to eat it all until we got home. I suppose this was his daily hot meal, as everything else had come straight from the can.

Our attendance at the Broadway meant that we met some of our neighbours, including one guy who had built a boat in his kitchen. Unfortunately it now took up his entire kitchen and he'd realised that he'd never be able to get it out of the room, even if he removed the large sash window. The last I'd heard, he'd asked a builder friend to consider removing the entire back wall of his house to release the boat.

If we ever went to something on at the university in the evening, we usually made sure we got the last bus or occasionally we'd walk the four or five miles home. One such walk came after our attendance at a Jam concert at the old Queen's Hall in Leeds. We'd managed to get tickets but were alarmed to read in the music press that a group of students had been beaten up at one of their gigs, for being students. We toyed for a while with the idea of not going and then came up with the idea of dressing up, so as not to look like students. This was easier said than done. What did students look like anyway and how do you dress to not look like one? It was like a friend who is a policeman. He was asked to go undercover one evening in a night club and was told not to look like 'an off-duty copper.' Whatever he tried on, his outfit screamed 'off-duty copper.' I'm sure any potential drug dealers at the club thought, 'I'd better avoid that off-duty copper and do my deals somewhere else!' Anyway, I'm sure the non-students in Leeds were spoilt for choice for students to bash; there must have been hundreds of us in attendance. It turned out to be one of the best gigs I've ever seen. The Jam were supported by The Vapors, who were flying high in the charts with 'Turning Japanese' and were very well received, but when the headliners finally took to the stage, the crowd were at fever pitch. After the first number, Paul Weller greeted us all with, 'I'm f**king pissed off!' and the cheer was even louder. Sadly, the band split up two years later and the old Queen's Hall was demolished in 1989 to be replaced by a car park.

We always had a good laugh in Beeston and one of the best came at Julian's expense. Julian fancied himself as a handyman and if anything went wrong in the house, he'd be the one who would be the keenest to sort it out. This was his Achilles heel and we set out to exploit it. One evening we plotted to scare the life out of him, by tricking him to go down into our vast cellar, which contained the fuse box and junk on one side and an old table tennis table on the other. Unbeknown to Julian, Jez had purchased a really life-like mask of the Russian president, Leonid Brezhnev, and hid himself in the cellar. At a pre-arranged time, he flicked the switch and stopped all the electricity in the house. It worked like a treat.

Mark and I were watching TV and hoovering in the lounge when Jez threw the switch. Julian immediately bounded into the lounge.

'The electricity's off!' I said, stating the obvious.

'It might be a fuse gone,' replied Julian, 'I'll sort it. Have you got a torch?'

For some reason a torch was already out on the fireplace, so I passed it over. Julian switched it on, opened the door to the cellar and descended slowly down the stone steps, followed by Mark and I, barely suppressing our laughter. He turned to the right and shone the torch over towards the fuse box. As soon as we reached the floor of the cellar, a figure dressed in an old trench coat and looking remarkably like Leonid Brezhnev, gave out a low groan and slowly raised himself from his horizontal position on the table tennis table. Julian quickly turned the torch to the other side of the cellar,

'Who's there?' he asked in a quivering sort of voice and as the beam of the torch alighted on the president's impassive face, he let out an almighty scream, dropping the torch as he ran out of the cellar, taking two steps at a time. Mark and I erupted into laughter and we raced after him, slowly followed by Leonid, whose face showed no signs of any emotion after his ordeal. Julian, on the other hand, needed a couple of drinks before he saw the funny side.

It was through Julian that I met my next house-mates, Jan and Fiona. We had an end-of-year party at the house in Beeston and Julian invited his new girl-friend, Jan and a large group of her fellow nurses. I got talking to her friend, Fiona and within ten minutes had fixed up an appointment to view a vacant room in her and Jan's flat near the university. I was planning to stay in Leeds over the summer to work on my dissertation and was keen to find somewhere else to live, as we were giving up the Tempest Road house. Two weeks later, I had moved in. If I had a great deal to thank Julian for, Jez owed him even more. He and Fiona quickly became an item and to date they have been happily married for thirty years.

Living with nurses quickly reminded me of one of the shadows hanging over Leeds at the time – the Yorkshire Ripper. On my first day in Leeds, the university organised for every new student to attend a short fifteen minute police presentation on the Ripper. They made students clear of the dangers we faced as young people (girls in particular, obviously) and played the chilling 'Wearside Jack' tape, which they were convinced was the real voice of the Ripper. We were to listen to the tape and say if we recognised the voice, or listen out around Leeds for anyone who sounded like it and immediately report them to the police. Nobody knew that the tape was a fake and the real Ripper had already been questioned and investigated by police, but released on account of his voice. Living with Jan and Fiona and later other nurses revealed that they had been given a similar talk and tape presentations and that there was a rumour going round that the next victim was going to be a nurse. As a result, they tended to stick together, get lifts from each other or stay at another nurse's house or even at the nurse's hostel at the Leeds General Infirmary, so as not to be left alone. On some mornings, I'd get up early to walk one of them to work, if their shifts did not coincide or they were unable to secure a lift. There was even a rumour going round the university that the next victim was going to be a male, so the walk back home from the hospital at 6 a.m. was often done very quickly.

When the Leeds University student, Jacqueline Hill's body was found near Lupton flats in November 1980, the fear became even more palpable and everybody was on edge. My friend Nick was crossing Hyde Park one Saturday afternoon when he was attacked (and hospitalised) by a mob of demonstrating women who saw him as a potential threat.

The most extreme reaction came after a night of clubbing in Leeds. A group of female students noted that one of their friends was missing. The police were called and their initial investigation showed that she was last seen talking to Mike, a young male student with a Geordie accent (a bit like Wearside Jack?). Some of the lads at the club knew where Mike lived and willingly passed on the information. Within thirty minutes a SWAT team had descended on Mike's bed-sit, broken down his door and discovered the girl sat astride a naked Mike in the throes of ecstasy. At least they would have something to tell their grandkids. A few months later, when the police finally arrested Peter Sutcliffe, the whole of Leeds and Yorkshire breathed a huge sigh of relief.

The pubs were more packed than ever and people felt safe enough to walk home in the dark. On one occasion, I was returning home after closing time at the Hyde Park and stepped into the gutter to avoid two men and a woman, obviously the worse for wear, staggering towards me. I'd stepped back onto the pavement when the girl let out a shout and I turned towards her,

'Oi! What do you think of this?' she slurred as she pulled up her t-shirt to reveal that she wasn't wearing a bra.

'They look like tits – only smaller!' I shouted and the two drunken men collapsed in laughter. They soon collapsed in pain too, as the woman set about them urging them to do something about the insult. I last heard her shout 'F**k off!' as I disappeared into the distance, not bothering to check if the remark was made to me or her drinking companions.

In all, I spent five happy years in Leeds. The B.A. course was swiftly followed by a one-year M.A. before enrolling on the PGCE course to get my teaching qualification. I had hoped to study for a Ph.D., but after a year trawling through all the 1832 editions of the Leeds Mercury and Leeds Intelligencer newspapers to uncover the actions of Michael Thomas Sadler during the first post-Reform Act election campaign in Leeds, I'd come to the conclusion that there was more to life than research. Who really cared that people - allegedly sponsored by one of Sadler's opponents - threw slates at him from the roof of Leeds Town Hall whilst he was addressing the hustings? When the highlight of your long day of investigation in the Brotherton Library is visiting the archaic toilet in the recesses of the basement and reading the scholarly graffiti, you know that you need to get out. It was here where I first came across –

'To be, or not to be.' (Shakespeare)
'To be is to do.' (Socrates)
'To do is to be.' (Sartre)
'Do be do be do.' (Sinatra)
'Scooby Dooby Do.' (Do)
'Yabba Dabba Do' (Flintstone)
In the same cubicle you could also read,
'One would have thought with all this wit,
Shakespeare had come here for a shit!'
Another scribbler had added,
'One would have thought with all this smell,

He'd dropped his f**king guts as well!'

They were hardly works of great literature, but they made me raise a smile and think to myself that if I found this to be the 'highlight' of my working day, I needed to get out more. Accordingly, I applied for a teacher training (or Post-Graduate Certificate of Education course, to give it its proper title) course at the Department of Education at Leeds University, still on campus and secured a teaching practice at the old Leeds Grammar School for Boys, which was in fact the closest school to the university and about two minutes from my new flat - so I was really broadening my horizons.

They say that location is everything and with this 'new' flat, it was certainly the case – it certainly had no other redeeming features. I'd had to move out of my previous flat (when one of my flatmates had to leave for Japan suddenly to nurse her brother who had been seriously injured in a car accident) and had chosen the new one, simply because it was a short move from the old one. This new 2-bedroomed flat boasted a tiny kitchen, a shared bathroom with the other two flats in the house and a new flatmate, another Dave. This guy was an Engineering student who announced on my first viewing of the spare room that he 'did a bit of pot', but would keep to his room when doing so. When I moved in he offered me a spliff and when I declined, showing him my asthma inhaler as an excuse, he pointed out that he could bake some cakes with it in if I preferred – I didn't. Fortunately he spent most of his time at the university and seemed to go out a lot, so our paths rarely crossed. He did have quite a few druggy mates who always seemed to be calling round looking for him and appearing to get somewhat agitated when I told them he wasn't in. One such, Henry, who reminded me of 'Shaggy' from 'Scooby Do', was always accompanied by a small even shaggier dog, ironically named 'Shaggy', who appeared to be just as stoned as his owner. My belief that Dave probably did a tad more than a 'bit of pot' was confirmed when I returned home from the university late one afternoon to find a note addressed to 'Dave', shoved under the door. Failing to recognise the scrawl and forgetting that the flat contained two Dave's, I curiously opened the folded note to reveal,

'Dave,
      Need 1/2oz Lebanon urgent. Cash payment.
                                Henry (and Shaggy)'

I re-folded the note, left it on the floor and started to look for alternative accommodation the next day.

The other bad thing about the flat was the shared bathroom, which was housed on a sort of mezzanine landing one floor down and was quite simply, absolutely minging. If you wanted to have a hot bath, you had to put about 50p in 10p pieces in a meter outside the door. You then had to wait for up to an hour for the water to heat, keeping a look out to ensure no other cheeky git dived in before you. When it was deemed to be 'bath time', you would spring into action. There was no floor covering on the stairs or even in the bathroom, so footwear needed to be worn to avoid splinters from the filthy un-sanded floorboards. You would spend the first allocation of hot water attempting to clean the bath so that it reached an acceptable standard that you would feel reasonably safe to step into it. If you had worn clothes to the bathroom, you tended to take a bag to put them in to, so as to avoid leaving them on the darkly-stained floor. The bathroom always seemed to be freezing cold, due to the new badly –fitted, single-glazed and unpainted wooden windows (you could see large gaps all around them) and taking off your final clothes or bathrobe was always a shock. If you avoided getting a splinter in your foot in the last step from floor into bath, it was always a bonus. End of bath time, the process was carried out in reverse. I always tried to get the whole thing over as quickly as possible to get back to the comparative comfort and warmth of my bedroom.

It was from this salubrious establishment that a young and almost-clean trainee teacher reported for duty to the prestigious Leeds Grammar School for Boys. In 1982, the PGCE course required students to complete two blocks of teaching practice – one, a short paired-practice one afternoon a week for about four weeks and the second, a longer individual placement. For both practices, I got Leeds Grammar.

Prior to the first placement, I was paired with another History trainee, Paul, and we were asked to attend a preliminary short meeting with the Head of History at the school. I remember it being very brief and at the end, we were asked to plan a series of lessons for two classes – 'Chivalry and Knighthood' for Year 7 and 'The Russo-Japanese War of 1904-5, with particular emphasis on the Battle of Tsushima Strait', for Year 11. Paul and I smiled, said our goodbyes and as we left the building, turned to each other; our looks showed that we wondered what we had let ourselves in for. Once again, please remember this was in the days before the internet. Researching and teaching 'Chivalry' was manageable but neither of us had ever heard of 'the Russo-Japanese War', let alone the

'Battle of Tsushima Strait.' When we returned to the university the next day, we asked fellow trainees, none of whom had a clue – they'd been asked to prepare lessons on more common themes like the Tudors or World War One. We scoured the Education library and resource centre for anything on Russia and Japan before trawling through the History section of the main university library and ended up having to use 'graduate- standard' texts to piece together a basic outline for us to develop, simplify and teach. Many hours of collaborative research and practice later, we were ready to face bands of well-behaved students, eager to further their knowledge of 20th century Russo-Japanese relations.

After the initial shock on the paired teaching, the individual placement passed much more smoothly and quickly. I was given a timetable of History and English lessons and let loose on the unsuspecting students. As I left my flat on the first morning, I passed a group of LGS sixth-formers having a crafty fag at the top of my road. I shouted them a cheery 'Morning!' and walked the final hundred metres to the school gates. After a couple of weeks, some of them began to recognise me as the 'new teacher' and started to reply to my morning greeting.

I was teaching about a fifty percent timetable and had Wednesday afternoons at the university for lectures and planning. Most of us used the Education Resources Room where you could buy acetate sheets to write on for the overhead projector, practice writing on a blackboard and get access to the state-of-the-art Banda machine. These machines were like manual photocopiers – you wrote your information on a stencil or 'Banda sheet', attached it to the drum of the Banda and then passed solvent through it. You cranked the handle and a paper copy of the original would be spat out. You could make them multi-coloured but the colour was never the same as the original – so the 'red' was always 'pink'. A skilled 'Banda Master' could probably turn out fifty copies in a minute, dependent on hand-cranking ability and amount of solvent in the machine. In these pre-mass-photocopying days, teachers grew skilled in making multiple copies (usually in a strange purple colour) from their pristine hand-written documents. You had to be very careful not to make a mistake on the original, as the carbonated backing sheet would pick it up and reveal any change faithfully in all reproductions. There was the added danger of staining your clothes with the pungent solvent, or even getting high. I recall one teacher nearly strangled himself when his tie got caught in one. I grew to become quite proficient in the multi-coloured Banda, but was fortunate that LGS was way ahead of the game and had its own efficient reprographics department who would do black-and-white photocopying for you given twenty-four hours' notice.

There's not much to say about the teaching placement. In those days you had only one visit from your tutor during your short stay and individual formal lesson observations from members of the department were deemed unnecessary. Quite often the host teacher would disappear from the classroom and leave you alone to face the students, most of whom were exceptionally well behaved. An older staff member told me that if he ever faced any discipline problems with students, he would threaten to phone home. This, he told me, would 'put the willies up' most students, whose parents were forking out thousands of pounds on private education and would not be impressed with Little Johnny kicking off and wasting their money. His other piece of advice was less useful – 'if you grabbed a student by their sideburns and lifted them up and down, it caused excruciating pain, but left no bruising.'

Fortunately, I did not have to resort to either tactic and managed to complete my time at LGS without any major problems. The students were a great bunch and I received a number of gifts from them when I left, including bottles of wine and whisky and (inevitably) the 1983 favourite, a 'Bernard Matthews' Turkey Roast'. Nowadays, I'd probably have to decline the presents and inform the Head Teacher – a sad reflection of the times.

After the main placement, we returned to the university and completed various lectures, seminars and pieces of written coursework, as well as multiple job applications. One of my tutors was the renowned Bronte scholar and thoroughly nice man, Brian Wilks. He gave great tutorials in his large room in the Education Department and for our final meeting promised a party. On the final day, we arrived to find a note on the door saying that we were to let ourselves in and help ourselves to the food and drink he'd provided as he would not be able to make it as he had sliced the top of his finger off in a kitchen accident. We did as requested and some guy left him a note saying that he had received an urgent telephone call during our tutorial and that he was to ring the number we supplied as soon as possible. If he did ever do this, the phone would have been answered with something like,

'Chapel Allerton Artificial Limb Centre, can I help you?'

I hope that his injury wasn't all that serious and that he took the joke in the spirit it was intended. After the meeting we all said our sad farewells to each other and we never saw Wilksy again.

The main business of the final term though was getting a job. Every Friday morning I would walk into the university and collect a copy of the Times Educational Supplement, as this was the only real way to find out about most teaching vacancies. I would head to one of the bars, buy a coffee and settle down with red pen in hand to trawl through the various lists. The jobs could come under 'History', 'Humanities', 'Local Authority', 'Individual School' or even by age range. You could tell if it was going to be a good week by the thickness of the Times Ed. I wasn't fussy. I applied for jobs in state or private schools all over the country. Sometimes you had to write off for an application form whilst other schools asked for a letter of application and a CV. I'd typed out a basic CV which I could use for most jobs, but all application forms and letters of application had to be done by hand and took hours. I sent away for details of at least ten jobs per week and probably sent off a minimum of eight actual applications per week. As Easter approached more and more jobs appeared, more and more were applied for and I started to get called for interview.

My first invitation for interview came from a school in Somerset, close to Bridgwater. To make the 9a.m. start I had to travel the day before and so I booked a room in a local pub. The train journey went without incident and when I got off at Bridgwater, I left the station looking for a bus stop and/or timetable. I found neither. I returned to the station and at the ticket desk asked,

'Excuse me. Could you tell me the time of the next bus to Langport?'

'That'd be Thursday, boy!'

'What?'

'Thursday's market day, see. You should have kept on the train to Taunton and got the bus to Langport from there.'

'But isn't Taunton further from Langport than Bridgwater?'

'Yes, but Taunton's got a bus!'

I waited an hour for the next train from Bridgwater (12 ½ miles from Langport) to Taunton (14 ½ miles from Langport) and managed to (just) catch the full-to-bursting last bus of the day back to Langport at 4.30 p.m. Conversations at the pub that night made me realise that if I actually got the job, a weekend away from Langport would be almost an impossibility if I had to rely on public transport. I considered withdrawing before the interview but knew that if this was the case, I wouldn't be able to claim any expenses, and the rail fare and overnight accommodation didn't come cheap for a poverty-stricken student. Fortunately I didn't need to worry. In spite of one senior staff member putting his hand on my knee and saying that he thought we could work well together, the job was given to one of the other candidates. I stifled a cheer and handed over my expenses form.

Two further failures at interview followed. A lovely posting at an all-girls' school on the Wirral (where they paid out expenses straight away from a vast hoard of cash kept in an ancient school safe) and one best avoided at a mixed comprehensive in North Yorkshire (where the five candidates were not given a tour of the school and were kept in a large room without any refreshments for three hours when not being interviewed). My application forms must have been OK though, for three further offers for interview arrived in the post and conveniently they fell on three consecutive days. The final two were over the Pennines in Lancashire, but the first was somewhere between Dewsbury and Wakefield in a place called Horbury. I'd never heard of it, but was willing to give it a try.

'Fortified Settlement in the Marsh'

As I sat on the bus from Leeds Bus Station to the unknown 'Horbury', little did I know that I was about to make the biggest career choice of my life. I remember the bus stopping in a place called 'Ossett' and a strange sense of calm and familiarity swept over me. I'd never been there before, yet somehow I was convinced that this was to be a big part of my future. I couldn't stop thinking, 'I'm going to live here when I get the job in Horbury.' There was not a shred of doubt or hesitation. It was one of those crystal clear moments when the world seems to stop for a moment and whispers to you, 'This is it!'

I'd experienced something similar a few years before when I first saw my future wife, Mary, sitting in the front of a Leeds University minibus. I thought to myself, 'I like the look of her. She could be 'The One'. I don't like the look of her boyfriend though!' We were about to go on a university History trip to Germany and I would try to engineer it so that we got the chance to talk to each other. What's even stranger was that on the same day, Mary told her friend (a girl with short hair who I'd mistakenly identified as 'the boyfriend') that she was convinced that we would be married some day – and we had barely said more than a few words to each other.

Her friend rightly pointed out that this was simply ridiculous. I'd not even asked her out, for goodness sake (it would take me at least another month to pluck up the courage for that); yet she was right.

This overwhelming feeling of utter conviction was with me as the bus trundled into Horbury and the driver told me this was the place to alight. Any vestige of nervousness had disappeared – it was inevitable that the job was mine. When I arrived I discovered that one candidate had already been interviewed the day before (and by all accounts was odds-on to get the job), one had withdrawn and that left just me and a girl who had just completed her first year of teaching at another local school, to be interviewed. In effect, I was third favourite, but this was not on my mind after my 'Epiphany.'

The tour of the school and meeting of key staff did little to shake my conviction and the interview could not have gone any better. In those days, you were not required to teach a lesson or do any paper exercises and you were told of the outcome (and offered face-to-face feedback) immediately after the decision was reached. I waited calmly in the office of the 'Senior Mistress' and chuckled to myself when I heard through the paper-thin walls of the next-door gents' toilet, one of the old governors tell another mid-wee, 'Well, I liked the bloke – he had red cheeks and smiled.'

So there you have it – smile and (if necessary) apply rouge to be sure of landing your dream job. Within fifteen minutes of the end of my interview, I was re-called and offered the post. My acceptance was immediate and they showed me my provisional timetable for the next year. Newly-Qualified Teachers (NQTs) today have it easy – my timetable covered seven different subjects taught in seventeen (yes, that's 17) rooms stretching all over the school, as well as being a form teacher for a Year 2 class. I was to teach History, English, Integrated Humanities, Latin, Music, Religious Education and European Studies. It looked daunting on paper, but at the time I was just delighted to get the job.

When September arrived, I had bought and moved into a house (in Ossett, of course) and planned as best as I could in those pre-Internet days. I relied heavily on any available textbooks and the widely-varying support of the seven different departments. History was fine. I got on well with the Head of Department, Steve, and he produced long-term lesson plans and recommended the appropriate textbooks. He was also in charge of the school's two video players and had a wide range of videos for almost every History topic on the school's syllabus. You had to book the video players a week in advance and then had to push or carry it to the area of the school you were in – quite a challenge when you are also taking a pile of exercise books, textbooks and sundry equipment to one of your seventeen allocated rooms.

English was a different matter. For my Year 1 class, I was told to read 'The Magician's Nephew' by C.S. Lewis and give them comprehensions from 'Art of English 1'. Year 3's were to read 'The Pigman' by Paul Zindel and do comprehensions from 'Art of English 3'. When I asked about my Year 4 class, the teacher proffered a battered copy of 'Art of English 4' and I could guess the rest. For a non-English specialist, I felt I was stitched up like a kipper and I must admit I sometimes struggled to plan series of lessons. As my friend Colin used to say, 'Planning? -that's what corridors are for!' When I look back, my first year of teaching was pretty awful and to be honest there was little outside support or monitoring, unlike today.

As an NQT, I was asked to attend a two-day residential in the palatial surroundings of Woolley Hall and received one half-day inspection visit from somebody in Wakefield LEA.

There's not much to say about the residential. I attended with Horbury's three other NQTs, (Nick, Ian and Sue) and we were talked at for two days. The highlight was undoubtedly being regaled with some great stories by Gervase Phinn, but the nadir was undoubtedly some guy with a guitar brought in by the authority to teach us how to meditate. I was seated next to Ian (a Music teacher) who I could hear flinch every time the guitarist played a bum note (and there were plenty to go at). We were asked to close our eyes and relax, but with Ian whispering, 'that should have been an 'F,'' or 'Tune the f**ker!' achieving a state of nirvana was an impossibility. The best parts of the course were the camaraderie with the other teachers, the food and the cheap bar at the end of the day.

One of the meals was a whole salmon which was served up on a platter to share on a table for about twelve. Unfortunately, many of the delegates were put off by the fact that the whole salmon did include the head and somewhat staring eyes. Nick tried to lighten the mood and managed to find a way of manipulating the salmon's mouth with his fork. We began a conversation which included as many fish puns as possible.

'Good cod man! Look at the skate of me – I feel a little eel.'

'Tuna, you sound a little tench. Sorry, I said that just for the halibut.'

'Did salmon say something? Could you repeat that? I'm hard of herring.'

'On your pike!'

'I've been whiting for that one.' etc.

We thought it hilarious and were crying with laughter – I'm not so sure most people felt the same.

The inspection visit was a cracker – the Wakefield LEA guy turned up unannounced just after lunch on a Thursday and watched me teach the three afternoon lessons and register my Year 2 form – it was 1-5 in those days rather than 7-11. After registering 2 Matthews in the lower school building, the afternoon began with a considerable walk to teach 'the Battle of Trafalgar' to Year 3 (Set 3) History in a music classroom in a separate building at the other side of the site, followed by 'Moses leading the Exodus from Egypt' to a Year 1 class in a room on the third floor of the main building (where ironically I was also timetabled to teach my Music lesson the day before!) The nightmare continued with 'Agriculture in Sweden' to a group of Year 3 (Set 4) European Studies students (many of whom had also been educated in naval warfare by me earlier that afternoon), close to where I'd started the afternoon in the junior block.

At first all was well. The Year 3 History class listened to my story of the battle, analysed some sources and most of them started to produce a written report, impressing the inspector. Only Mark, my arch nemesis, preferred to give the inspector the 'evil-eye' rather than do any work and was starting to lose his patience and begin twitching when the bell sounded for the change-over. My Year 1 RE group were as keen as mustard, answering politely the questions they were asked and completing as much written work as humanly possible in a way only first-years can.

And then it was time for European Studies. This was a subject set up by the school to save the skins of the Modern Foreign Languages teachers. Any Year 3 student in the bottom set for French or Spanish would have one of their MFL lessons taught by a Humanities (usually Geography) teacher to educate them on the 'practices and lifestyles' of our European cousins – although this frequently took the form of worksheets on farming. As we neared the classroom, I could already discern some groans about wishing it was 'home time.' I quietened the students and asked them to go inside. They all went to their seats, except Mark. He turned his good eye on the inspector before swivelling it around to land on me,

'Hey up, who is this f**king wanker?' he snarled.

'Outside! - Now!' I shouted

A few choice words later and after threatening him with spending time with the Head and Deputy as well as phoning his mum, dad, gran, Mother Teresa, my Hell's Angel chapter and Uncle T Cobley, a chastened Mark returned to the lesson and I have to say, behaved impeccably. I apologised to the inspector and much to my relief, the lesson passed without further incident. The inspector was impressed with the way I'd dealt with Mark (he didn't see what I said to him outside the room) and pointed out the obvious when he noted that I had a difficult job as a wandering teacher. He shook his head in disbelief at the range of subjects I was expected to cover as well, but in a way the whole experience summed up my first year of teaching – it wasn't very good, but I got through it. As the headmaster was fond of saying, 'It's good for your development.'

What helped me get through all of this was the staff – it never ceases to amaze me the skill, patience and camaraderie that teachers have. It's almost like a 'We're all in it together/backs to the wall' sort of mentality and in the early years, I learned so much from every teacher I talked to. The staff room was the place to compare notes, swap stories and ask for advice. For teachers teaching in new school buildings (where the main staff room is usually replaced by multiple small department 'work rooms'), a staff room is simply that. It's a room for staff to relax in. It doesn't have writing desks in it and (in 1983) certainly doesn't have computers. You don't do marking in it or bring students in to complete their homework – it's your place of refuge to relax in before, during and after a tiring teaching day. It contains comfortable chairs or sofas, coffee tables to put your coffee mugs on and there is usually somebody to make your drink for you, certainly at break times. Some staff would arrive early for school to socialise in it, some would spend their entire lunch hour (and in those days it was a full hour) here and others would have 'an hour after school' to wind down. It was the place to do the crossword, knit a jumper, have a fag, fill in your pools coupon, write your shopping list, play cards and put the world to rights. Many staff had been there for years, had their own preferred seats and happily shared their experiences, warning you about certain students, passing on their wisdom or simply chatting. When I first arrived at Horbury, the room was almost split into two sides – the window side for the ladies and the smokers and the corridor side for the men. Students would be told that they could only ever go to this room if there was an emergency and a sign on the door instructed them to knock twice and wait. I remember a first year student once knocked on the door and poked his head inside to see if a certain member of staff was in. There was nearly a riot. It was like the House of Commons during an unruly debate. Shouts of 'Get out!' and 'Stranger!' were quickly followed by at least three teachers hurtling towards the door, anxious to lay hands on the unfortunate visitor – he wouldn't make that mistake again.

Occasionally visitors would be brought into the staff room to pass a few minutes before a meeting, but it wasn't really the 'done thing' and it could be frowned upon if you brought your own visitor into the room. The appearance of a 'stranger' usually resulted in a 'toning down' of conversations or even a few moments of complete silence as we scanned the unfortunate visitor before interrogating them.

In my first few years, one familiar visitor was a partially –sighted man who came to do a talk to groups of younger students about raising money for 'Guide Dogs for the Blind'. He didn't have a guide dog himself and usually was able to get around quite effectively with the aid of his white stick. On one occasion he felt the need to use the toilets before his talk and asked for directions. We explained that it was the second door on the right down the corridor and that the room had two urinals and two toilet cubicles (or 'traps' as we called them). We offered to show him the way but he refused, saying it was quite alright, he'd be fine. Meanwhile, one of the other male teachers, Eric, was quietly relieving himself at one of the two urinals. He heard the outer door open and close and the next thing he knew something was poking him hard in the backside, forcing him to suffer splash-back.

'You dirty bastard!' yelled Eric (believing it to be one of his mates, playing one of the latest pranks).

He spun round, saw the white stick and immediately realised that it was an accident.

'Oh! I'm really sorry. I thought it was my mate, Tom.'

The visitor had been so shocked by the initial outburst that he clicked with his cane a path into the nearby cubicle and in a (blind) panic had somehow managed to get himself stuck in it, unable to work out where the door handle or even the door was. Eric continued to proffer his apologies and eventually, with Eric's help, the guy was able to calm himself down and leave the toilets safely, without ever using them. When Eric finally confessed to the rest of the staff room what had happened and how he blamed Tom, we were not sympathetic. The visitor returned on future occasions, but he never asked to use the toilet again. On the few occasions he re-appeared in the staff room when Eric was there, Eric would move away from his mates and cower in silence over the other side of the staff room with the smokers. The frequent quips of 'You're very quiet today, Eric; are you not sitting with us?' were usually met with a two-fingered response.

The staff room was usually a place of laughter and merriment and pranks were common. On one occasion, one member of staff brought in a rubber spider and attached a long line of dark elastic to it. He proceeded to lower it out of the staff room window so that it would hover and then bounce up and down outside the window of the room below – the headmaster's office. Unfortunately, he did not realise that the head was in a meeting with the Chairman of Governors, where they were engaged in a serious disciplinary with a fifth-former and his bemused parents, who were following the up-and-down movement of the spider and didn't seem to be grasping the seriousness of their son's predicament. The headmaster did not see the funny side of it and the teacher then had to attend their own disciplinary.

On another occasion, I was the victim of the pranksters. I was gaining a reputation for imitating different accents and doing silly impersonations and could be persuaded to take on the role of the entertainer at the drop of a hat – come on, you know that all teachers are really failed wannabe stand-up comedians. One of my most recent efforts was an imitation of a bull, a sort of cross between Bully from Bullseye and Kevin Costner's imitation of a buffalo in 'Dances with Wolves'. One lunch time I was quietly reading the paper when one of the lads piped up,

'Come on, Dave. Give us your 'Bully' impression. Anyone who's never seen this – you're in for a treat.'

After a split second of protest I'd got onto all-fours, inserted my wedding ring up my right nostril and proceeded to scratch around the staff room carpet, snorting and bellowing. The crowd was in raptures – I'd never seen them so animated. Al was crying with laughter, Tom was going so red that I thought he was having a heart attack and Eric was spraying soup all over the place. This was incredible – I'd had a good reaction in the past but this was by far the best audience appreciation I'd ever had. 'I must be really good,' I thought. I continued to scratch, grunt and bellow, getting louder all the time. After a few minutes, Al managed to compose himself enough to tap me on the shoulder and point at something behind me. I turned slowly to catch sight of one of the young female art candidates, who had somehow entered the room without my knowledge. I'd made a fool of myself in front of a stranger who sported a face flushed with embarrassment and a large shiny nose-ring, remarkably similar to the gold wedding ring I was quickly removing from my nasal passage.

'Sorry, I didn't realise, I mean it wasn't, sorry,' I mumbled and I turned to look at my so-called friends, high-fiving each other and still laughing freely.

'W**kers!' I hissed.

I felt sorry for the young lass who thankfully was called away for interview within a matter of minutes. She can't have been that rattled because she actually got the art job and rose through the ranks to become Assistant Head at Horbury. She was even my line manager for a time. Of course, the Bully impersonation has been cut from the act, although the re-runs of Bullseye on Challenge TV could merit a recall. The whole episode should have taught me a valuable lesson, but it probably didn't. After a self-imposed exile on the smokers' side of the staff room for a few days, life quickly returned to normal.

The mention of smokers in the staff room just shows how times have changed. In the early 1980's nobody would ever think of banning smoking in communal areas. The smokers just sat near the windows for ventilation and nobody bothered them. Most of them smoked cigarettes, although some preferred small cigars and Steve, the Head of History, was even known to enjoy a pipe.

I enrolled in his evening class at the school on local history to try and make sense of my new environment. Useful local knowledge like 'Horbury' is in Domesday Book and means 'fortified settlement in the marsh' and that the parish of Sitlington (Sitlington Round Table take note) used to be written as 'Shitlington' or 'Shyttelington' came second to my learning of how to engage and enthuse an audience. Steve was a remarkable teacher and I owe him a lot.

In the 1980's there were other differences too. Remember that corporal punishment wasn't actually outlawed in state schools until 1986, although I cannot recall it ever being used at all at Horbury (I started in September, 1983). Steve used to have an old white gym pump/training shoe which he kept menacingly on the top of his blackboard. He'd nicknamed it 'Sweaty Betty' and rumour had it that he marked it with a swastika every time it had been used. Steve was only happy to promote this myth and liked to add increasingly colourful swastikas every few months.

Sexism was rife as well. All formal registers and set lists had to be written out in alphabetical order with boys at the top and girls at the bottom. Whereas boys were encouraged to take up the tough manly subjects of Woodwork and Metalwork, girls were assigned Typing (sometimes re-named 'Office Practice'), Home Economics (Cooking) and Housecraft.

Covering lessons (even by newly-qualified teachers) for absent colleagues was the norm and one a week was probably the average requirement. Quite often you'd be faced by a wall of unfamiliar faces that were only too happy to 'test out the new guy' and if you got one of the practical subjects, you felt that you took your life into your hands.

Rural Studies was particularly daunting. This was a subject that students were engineered into if it was felt they were too weak and/or too disruptive for the core science programme. It was taught in a temporary classroom on the edge of the site, away from the rest of the school. It had a greenhouse, an allotment area and some small outbuildings for an array of chickens, rabbits and a goat. Cover lessons here normally meant students completing written tasks, as animal and plant husbandry were alien to the vast majority of staff. After surviving a lesson here, you always regarded the regular teacher, Andy, with full respect. Less sensitive staff labelled his subject 'Rabbit Stroking' as this seemed to be the main student task for much of the year. In autumn though, the students donned their fluorescent jackets and did leaf sweeping as well. On one occasion the Year 5 students were engaged on this task for the last lesson on a Friday. They were scattered around the school site and the teacher had asked them to return their forks and jackets to the classroom when the bell went. When he returned with a couple of the stragglers a few minutes after the bell, he did a quick check and realised four forks were missing. Cursing to himself, he left the classroom to search for his missing tools. He didn't have to go far. A short distance away he spied a small mound of leaves with four forks sticking out from the top. As he approached, the pile of leaves started to move and a muffled sound could be heard. Andy quickly moved to the pile and when he brushed the pile aside, he uncovered the smallest of his Year 5 students, pinned down with the garden forks at the ankles and wrists. It was certainly a good job that he had done the stock check on his tools.

Many students got a lot out of these lessons, but none more so than an SEN student, who I'll call Mike. Mike took a particular shine to Molly, the school goat and visited her at least three times a day. He brought scraps from home for her and usually fed her before school, at break time and lunch. He would sit and talk to the goat for as long as he could, preferring her company to that of any student. On one Friday night, the teacher discovered to his horror that Molly was dead. He immediately thought of Mike and how distraught he'd be and quickly concocted a plan. He managed to contact a goat owner the next day and was able to select a replacement for Molly. He thought about what Molly looked like and tried to get as close a match as possible. By the time Mike hopped off the school bus on Monday morning and made his way with his scraps of food to the goat enclosure, Molly's doppelganger was in situ. The teacher looked on nervously as Mike began his conversation, telling Molly what he'd been up to at the weekend. He approached cautiously and asked,

'Everything alright, Mike?'

'It's Molly, there's something different about her.'

'What do you mean?' enquired the teacher, thinking he was about to be rumbled.

'She's a different colour!'

'Oh. Goats sometimes change their coat in winter. It's quite normal!' retorted Andy, as quick as a flash and nothing more was ever said.

Andy was a kind, caring and skilled teacher doing a very difficult job, working with some of the most vulnerable and challenging students. I remember him once getting a piece of written work from one of the most menacing Year 5 students. It was about 'rabbit handling' (of course) and was a full page of A4 of 'Hold the f**king f**ker making sure that the f**king bastard........' I'm sure you get the picture. Andy was supposed to mark this for the 16-plus examination. He sought the advice of the Head of Year, who told him,

'Give it six out of ten. That's the most the lad's written – ever. He's written it the way he talks.'

In the end, the teacher never had to mark it as the student was withdrawn from school after he hot-wired his probation officer's car and drove it into a brick wall. The police also found him in possession of a plan to rob a local brewery of hundreds of its bottles and then return them to the same place to claim the bottle deposit refund for returns – I never found out if the plan was written in the same style as the Rural Studies assignment. Unfortunately the Rural Studies course died out when Andy moved on to another job and when some psycho murdered all the chickens one night.

Other practical departments often deemed it 'too dangerous' for a cover teacher to carry out practical sessions, which could involve operating the large and dangerous machinery and power tools. This could lead to a mutiny by the students and a refusal to work. For some reason, taking a cookery lesson was deemed as acceptable only with the older students, so long as you didn't let them leave a mess at the end of the session or set fire to the classroom. The most relaxing cover though was Typing. This was normally taught in a double lesson and if you were lucky enough to catch the second lesson, you'd turn up to find 30 girls seated behind their machines, tapping away. They just typed, smiled and when they finished their assignment, glided noiselessly to the front of the room to collect their next piece of work. The 'tap tap, bing' of the machines was strangely therapeutic and could almost be deemed soporific. I certainly fell asleep in at least one of my covers there.

Sometimes students complain about their teachers to other members of staff who obviously remain professional and dismiss the complaints before telling their mates what has been said. I remember one crusty old teacher who came in for a lot of stick from the students. I never really talked to this guy as he was in a different department and tended to chain-smoke in the corner of the staff room. Students complained that they could never understand a word he said. The only conversation I had with him was when I was acting as a union representative and had to ask him for his home address for the central files. Even though I asked him to repeat it three times, all I managed to understand was 'Castleford', so when I returned the form to the union, I wrote on it – 'Still living in Castleford!'

The guy used to travel to school in a beat-up hatchback and staff that travelled in the same direction as him, frequently complained of being cut-up, subjected to under-taking and being witness to road rage directed against them. Accordingly we spread the word that the teacher was actually a stock-car driver who had earned a living at the Odsal track in Bradford, before being banned for dangerous driving. The stock-car, of course, was no longer used at the track, so had been 'spruced up' for the daily commute and 'family living.'

Students also used to complain that another teacher had a body odour problem. One lad got himself into bother when at the end of a lesson, he addressed the teacher,

'Hey up, sir. Are you doing anything this weekend?'

'No, I don't think so.'

'In that case, get a f**kin' bath!'

In the early days the school was divided into a Lower School for the first two years (Y7 and Y8 in today's money), a Middle School (for Y9) and an Upper School (for Y10 and Y 11). Lower School was under the auspices of a crazy Scottish lady called Mary. She acted like a surrogate mum/gran for many of the smaller students and would always steal the show at the Year 1 Christmas party/disco when she entered the hall on a small tricycle dressed in shorts and a school blazer as Wee Jimmy Krankie. My most vivid memory of her though is at a Year 2 'Youth Wing Assembly'.

Every week, in addition to the Lower School assembly in the main hall, each of the two lowest year groups attended their own weekly assembly in the school's 'Youth Wing.' This was the venue for the evening youth clubs, as well as the fifth –form (Y11) common room. The young students were escorted by form staff into the lower-floor area and were asked to sit cross-legged on the floor. In the meantime the eight form teachers (including me) sat four to a bench and faced the other staff across a Formica table on a raised area. The assembly usually went along the lines of any notices followed by a presentation by a particular class and either a speech of praise or occasionally, condemnation from Mary. This time it was something different. Mary looked dazed and rather angry as she cut a swathe through the seated children and took up a position directly in front of the assembled staff. She had a jam jar in her hand which she placed on the table next to me before turning to face the students.

'No notices this week. I have a very serious matter to discuss with you,' she began.

The children looked at each other nervously and the staff shuffled in their seats.

'Does anyone know what this is?'

A young boy at the front raised his hand.

'It's a jam jar, miss.'

'Aye. It's a jam jar and it's used to hold jam.'

('Ten out of ten for 'Education by stating the bleedin' obvious!" I thought. What on earth was she doing? Had she finally lost the plot? Perhaps this was some new fund-raising activity she had devised which could be adapted by eager students? Maybe she was going to start a jam production line in the cookery department?)

'But on this occasion it's been used for something very different by a very sick boy!'

'The cleaners at this school work very hard for little thanks. Imagine their surprise when they found this jar in the boys' toilets with a jobby in it!'

(The way Mary had said 'Jobby' had an enormous effect on the staff. Andy let out a snort, Nick started to go red and I could feel a sort of uncontrollable shoulder shaking start to take control of me.)

'He then left this jobby right by the side of the toilet! What's wrang with using the proper toilet?

(We all knew this was a serious matter but more staff struggled to contain their emotions.)

'This person needs to be stopped before he does it again! Can you imagine somebody actually doing it?

(As somebody now mimed placing a jam jar under their backside, we could imagine it only too clearly. Andy's eyes were now streaming with tears, Nick was a sort of sweaty scarlet and I was having a self-induced asthma attack.)

Somehow none of the kids spotted what we were up to and after the end of Mary's tirade, (when she urged the culprit or any witnesses to pass on a name, so that the student could get psychiatric help) she walked out of the building, blissfully unaware of the mayhem she'd created. After the students had been dismissed, the staff could regain their composure, Andy and Nick making use of their handkerchiefs and me resorting to the Ventolin inhaler. 'The Phantom Shitter' went down in the annals (or should I say, anals) of Horbury History and we never did find out who it was. A few years later and an Upper School boy was caught having a dump in one of the displays at Rent-a-Tent in Horbury, but we did not have the forensic capabilities to connected him to the 'Jobby in the Jar' incident. Mary continued to say things which caused unplanned mayhem. When announcing in assembly that the young male PE teacher was starting a tennis club every Thursday night, she ended the news item by shouting to the aforementioned teacher standing at the back of the hall,

'Are you alright for balls, Mr Craig?'

The other member of the senior leadership who I had dealings with in my first year of teaching was Doreen, the Senior Mistress. She was in charge of all newly-qualified teachers and in those days that meant having a termly meeting and being there to pick up the pieces when things (inevitably) went wrong. There were no training programmes, no lesson observations and certainly no book scrutinies. I found Doreen to be thoroughly honest, thoroughly kind and thoroughly professional. She had the reputation of being extremely fierce and you certainly wouldn't want to cross her.

When I started at Horbury I was told a story about an ex-member of staff and his run-in with Doreen. According to a number of teachers, this guy - we'll call him Guy (but I honestly don't know the guy) – was hauled into Doreen's office early one Monday morning and accused of exposing himself in public. It doesn't sound good and certainly does Guy little credit. Apparently Guy had been entertaining his girlfriend over the weekend and went to see her off on to a train home from an almost deserted Wakefield Westgate Station late one Sunday evening. He saw her onto the train and started to walk away just before the train departed. He then had this idea that as there was nobody about and seemingly nobody on the train, instead of just waving his hand, he'd wave 'Little Guy' instead. As the train started to edge away, he unzipped and started to 'wave'. His girlfriend slowly passed him by and laughed at the joke, but in the next set of seats, previously un-noticed by Guy, the only other passenger on the train, Doreen, was staring out of the window. Guy and 'Little Guy' both froze and as he re-arranged himself, cursing his bad luck, he knew that he'd been caught out. He couldn't sleep that night and desperately tried to think of a way out. I think he pre-empted the call by presenting himself at Doreen's office as soon as he arrived at school the next day. The story he'd come up with was that it was an old joke he always played on his girlfriend by placing a hot dog sausage in his pants and making out that he was waving his manhood. He told Doreen he thought that his girlfriend was the only train passenger that night, apologised for any offence and assured her that he'd keep his sausages at home in future. Somehow he survived, but I think the trauma made him leave Horbury at the earliest opportunity and probably still lives with him today.

Fortunately I am 'cock-a-hoop' to report that I never found the need to wave my todger in public or purchase any cans of hot dog sausages to cover up such misdemeanours. As for Doreen, the matter was never 'raised' again – perhaps they should have 'erected' a statue in her honour.

My admiration for (and to be honest, fear of) Doreen increased immensely when she helped me out with a problem I was having with a particularly awkward second-year Latin student. It's quite strange that I had some really challenging classes and students in my probationary year (bottom set third year English, History and European Studies spring to mind), yet the one student I sought help with, was in a supposedly high-ability Latin class.

Paul was an able student who never quite reached his full potential – he would show 'only a modest willingness' to do work of any kind, as my mate Pete would say. He had been placed in top set English and thus had one Latin lesson with me each week (in an isolated portakabin converted into a science lab, of course) This was done to motivate him and give the teachers of the other sets a chance to deal with other troublesome students. You could say he was allergic to written work of any kind and would resort to a variety of imaginative strategies to entertain his fellow students, disrupt the lesson and above all, create havoc for the teacher. On this particular occasion, the Latin class were being enthralled by the continuing realistic adventures (in very basic Latin) of Caecilius and his Pompeiian family. Paul had already been warned about overly exaggerated yawns and occasional interjections of 'Boring!' I was asking one of the students to translate 'Caecilius est in villa' into English, when the silence was broken by an unmistakably loud voice exclaiming,

'Caecilius is a w**ker!'

I turned on Paul immediately.

'What did you say?' was the best I could come up with. 'Would you care to repeat that?'

'I never said owt,' he replied.

'Paul. I heard what you said. Everybody in the class heard what you said. I'm going to give you one chance to apologise for using such unacceptable language or I'll take the matter further,' I said, making it up as I went along.

'Looks like you're gonna have to take it further then,' he announced cheerfully.

I thought for a split second and then said calmly and sweetly,

'Go to the office of the Senior Mistress and tell her what you've just told me.' (After all she was in charge of all NQT's and just the day before had reminded me that I could always send to her any student who was causing me any problems.)

The colour quickly drained from Paul's face, but without saying a word, he left the classroom and headed towards main school. The class looked on in expectation and I continued with the Latin. A few minutes passed quite serenely before the real action began.....

The door to the 'lab' swung open and in walked Doreen, closely followed by an ashen-faced Paul. What happened next seemed so rehearsed; it was as if it was being acted out in a play:

Scene: *Mid-afternoon - a portakabin containing thirty one students seated in rows of desks/benches. A young teacher, Mr M, stands at the front reading Latin from an orange booklet and stops abruptly as the door creaks open stage left to allow Doreen, an aging senior teacher and a student, Pale Paul, to join the action. . . . .*

Doreen: Mr Matthews. Paul tells me you sent him to see me for no apparent reason. Is this correct?

Mr M: Not at all, miss. Paul was extremely rude in front of the whole class.

Doreen: Really! Are you sure you are not mistaken?

Mr M: Absolutely sure, miss!

Doreen: Where does Paul sit?

Mr M *(pointing to the only empty chair in the classroom)*: Over there, next to Michelle.

Doreen *(addressing the girl in the next seat)*: Did you hear what Paul said?

Michelle: Yes, miss.

Doreen *(addressing another girl in the seat immediately in front of Paul's)*: Did you hear what Paul said?

Sarah: Yes, miss.

Doreen *(addressing a boy in the seat immediately behind)*: Did you hear what Paul said?

Gary: Yes, miss.

Doreen *(clicking her fingers and pointing at Michelle)*: What did he say?

Michelle: Caecilius is a w**ker, miss.

Doreen *(clicking her fingers and pointing at Sarah)*: What did he say?

Sarah: Caecilius is a w**ker, miss.

Doreen *(clicking her fingers and pointing at Gary)*: What did he say?

Gary: Caecilius is a w**ker, miss.

Doreen *(spins to face Paul)*: You, laddie. Get out!

Doreen (to *Mr M, much more quietly)*: I'm so sorry, Mr Matthews. Nobody has to put up with that. Paul will be with me for the rest of the afternoon. Come and see me at the end of school.

Doreen and Paul exit.

An hour and a half later, I was in Doreen's office. Paul was still there. He looked completely different with tear-stained cheeks, a running nose and bloodshot eyes. He was standing, crying quietly in the corner, as Doreen explained,

'Paul and I have had a little chat. He is very sorry for his rude behaviour and even sorrier for telling lies to the both of us. He would like to offer you an apology.

'I'm...so....sorry, sir. It'll never...happen again!' he sobbed.

'Be sure it doesn't, laddie!' snapped Doreen, 'Now, do you catch a school bus?'

'No, miss. My mum is picking me up tonight,' replied Paul, starting to regain his composure.

'Well, dry your face. Sort yourself out! You're welcome to tell your mum about your behaviour today. She can come in to see me, if she likes. Now, get out. If I ever hear about you misbehaving again, it'll be a lot worse!'

I actually felt sorry for the lad. What could be worse than an hour and a half's telling off from Doreen? The next week, Paul returned to the lessons and his behaviour was exemplary. As time passed and the emotional scarring started to heal, Paul started to return to his old self. However, he was very careful not to over-step the mark and Caecilius was never accused of self-abuse again.

At Horbury, some head teachers often used to quote the old adage, 'we go the extra mile.' Sometimes this was used to justify to staff why some uncontrollable student continued to attend the school in spite of the fact that the vast majority of their teachers were tearing their hair out in frustration. One such student was Amy, who somehow had remained in school up to the end of her second year. I'm not sure what the formal explanation of her condition was, but to put it in simple terms, she was barmy – harmless, but barmy. Things came to a head at an end of year English competition, where students had to write and read out their work on a specific topic. The school took this seriously and the best three or four pieces from each English group were performed on stage in the main hall in a sort of 'literature festival' in front of all of the lower school and an outside judge. Amazingly, Amy had performed well within her English set and had been selected for the festival. All went well for the performance and after a little contemplation; the guest judge declared that Amy had indeed won. This is where things started to go horribly wrong. Having accepted her prize, she started a lap of honour around the hall, whooping and screaming before returning to the stage for a final bow. As the stage curtain closed and then re-opened to reveal the next four contestants, Amy could be seen peering round the curtain at the edge of the stage, waving to a few friends. It was then that she spotted her favourite teacher, Mr Roberts. She whispered loudly,

'Mr Roberts. . . . .Mr Roberts . . . . .I love you, Mr Roberts!'

She then proceeded to blow him big squelchy kisses and the audience laughed nervously. The Head of Lower School could take no more and warned Amy (now centre stage and proclaiming her love for Mr Roberts at full volume) that unless she got off stage there and then, she would be disqualified. This was like lighting the red touch paper and Amy increased her volume. She had to be physically removed from the stage by the Head of Lower School and as she was dragged past poor Mr Roberts, she blew her final few kisses to him. The teacher marched her right down the central aisle of the assembly hall to the main doors and out. As Amy struggled in the vice-like grip of the teacher, she could be heard to sing to the tune of 'Magic Moments',

'I'll never forget the smell of the sweat from under your armpits!'

Shortly after this, Amy moved to another school in the authority where she lasted less than two weeks; so perhaps we did go the extra mile. We certainly used to go the extra mile in Parents' Evenings which seemed to go on forever.

In the old days, Parents' Evenings were a nightmare. The school had one BBC computer which was used to scan in and produce a set of appointments for every teacher. Appointments could start as early as five o'clock and last up to half-past nine. Even if you only had about six or seven appointments, the computer would scatter them throughout the evening to ensure you stayed at least an extra hour or so longer than was actually needed. As time went on, the school abandoned the computer and staff were trusted to arrange their own appointments. Eventually, organising Parents' Evenings became one of the administrative tasks that I was given responsibility for, which meant that I had to stay at the school from the first appointment to the last. Although appointments officially ended at nine o'clock, many staff made later ones and some, who could talk for Britain, went way over their allotted time. Maths and English teachers were the worst, some bringing in exercise books to refer to in some detail and one even sharing the student's response to a range of complex mathematical questions on recent exam papers, within the allotted five minutes per appointment. Suffice it to say, they delayed parents from other appointments which angered both staff and parents. I think the latest ever was about a quarter past ten – we even struggled to make 'last orders' at the pub.

In the early years, students never attended the meetings, but often their attitude and behaviour was mirrored by their parents. I explained to one parent,

'Rob has difficulty in maintaining concentration for more than a few seconds and it's affecting his learning.'

'Sorry, what did you say?' was the response.

My favourite reaction though, comes courtesy of Whisky Walt. At his first ever Parents' Evening, he was trying to tread carefully around his comments about a problem student,

'I'm afraid Stuart is causing a few problems. He never completes classwork, refuses to do homework, shouts out in class and really shows no respect whatsoever.'

His father's reply was,

'Aye, lad. What you're trying to say is that he's a right bastard! And you're right.'

His wife just sat there red-faced with mouth gaping in astonishment.

Sometimes parents also showed their true colours when they used to write excuse letters to school. In the old days, before mobile phones, texts and e-mails, students were required to bring in a letter if they had had time off. Occasionally these would be written by the students themselves to cover up truancy or to get out of PE, but you had to be careful to check the files to match up the handwriting of parents before you accused a student of forgery. My Top 3 excuse letters of all-time were:

3. 'Russell was late to school after lunch yesterday, because he fell in a puddle, the stupid prat.'
2. 'Ian was off yesterday because he had dia dyer dierhere (previous three words crossed out) the shits'
1. 'Colin couldn't come to school on Monday because he was very upset. His gran is in hospital and his cat has gone missing. Steve Davis losing in the snooker at the weekend didn't help either.'

Notes like these would be passed around the staff room to the delight of all. Teachers were always eager to hear anything out of the ordinary, like what happened at the end of a Year 7 PE lesson in one of the early years of my career. Tony, a proper PE teacher and I had taken a group of students to the off-site rugby pitches for a lesson, as per the usual timetable. We'd carried down a large net full of rugby balls and had left them at the door of the changing rooms as we all went in to get changed. On our return, we were just in time to see two young lads (in their late teens, early twenties?) heading across the rugby field dragging the net of balls. We shouted after them, giving chase whilst the students gazed on in disbelief. In the end, we retrieved the net and most of the balls, but the lads had escaped with two or three of the better rugby balls. After the lesson and returning the students to main school, we decided to get in Tony's car and trawl the nearby estate and underpass where the lads had made off, to see if we could get anything else back. When we reached one end of the underpass, we got out of the car and started to walk through the fifty metre long tunnel. As soon as we started walking, we spied two figures, remarkably similar to the ball thieves. At that precise moment, one of them raised something in front of him and a small bang was heard, followed by a breath of air, as something zipped past my right ear. I looked at Tony and said something obvious like,

'They're shooting at us!'

We started to run in the direction we came from, just as another bang went off. By the time we had reached the relative safety of Tony's car, we had recovered enough composure to drive round to the other end of the tunnel. We never saw the gunslingers again, but we did manage to retrieve one more rugby ball, bobbing in the shallow water at the edge of the lagoon.

There used to be a bumper sticker that said, 'Rugby is a game played by men with odd-shaped balls.' This could have been proven if 'Dead-eye Dick' had been a tad more accurate in his shooting.

I've saved my most memorable story from my first year of teaching for last. It concerns a young, but experienced English teacher, Dave, who, like many of us, was having a few problems with a certain third-year class. He'd confided in this to one of his mates, a French teacher who devised a cunning plan. The next time he had this same dodgy class for a lesson, he started the ball rolling.

'What have you got for next lesson?' he asked one of the students.

'It's English – I hate English!'

'Who've you got for that?' continued the teacher.

On hearing Dave's name in the reply, the teacher sucked in his breath and shook his head from side to side.

'What's that all about, sir?' asked one lad.

'You don't want to mess with him, believe me!'

'What do you mean?'

'Er, nothing. I'm not supposed to say.'

By now he had the attention of the whole class. If they think they're going to uncover a secret or a bit of gossip, kids can't help themselves.

'Come on, sir!'

'You can trust us.'

'We wouldn't grass you up!'

This was playing perfectly into his hands. He pressed home his advantage.

'Well, alright then. But you must all promise not to tell anybody else about this or where you heard about it. Agreed?'

'Agreed!' shouted the kids, barely able to contain themselves.

'OK. Well here goes. Before he started at Horbury, your English teacher used to be a boxer. He doesn't like to talk about it because he had to give it all up, after he killed a guy in the ring. He changed his name and trained as a teacher instead, so he could do some good in the world and make up for his terrible past.'

'No?!?!'

'Yes – it's all true, but you must never EVER mention it to him. It could send him over the edge. Sometimes you can tell he is thinking about that fateful night, because he raises his eyes to the ceiling. That's when he's at his most dangerous.'

As the bell went for the lesson change, the students had built up a new respect and fear for their English teacher. It had to be true because they'd really had to force the French teacher to tell them the story and he'd sworn them to secrecy.

In English they got on with their work and eyed the boxer cautiously. Dave had been pre-warned about the tale and was only too happy to play along. The first half of the lesson passed in an almost eerie silence, until one student cracked,

'Excuse me, sir. Is it true that you used to be a boxer?'

'What?' asked Dave

The student repeated his question, this time a little more nervously, if that was possible.

'Did you use to be a boxer?'

'Yes! But I don't want to talk about it!' shouted Dave, and with a horrified look on his face, he slowly raised his eyes to the ceiling.

The kids were hooked. He was staring at the ceiling and clearly was thinking about the unfortunate opponent he'd killed in his murky past. From that day on, Dave never had any problem with any of his students. At the first sign of any hint of insurrection, he'd simply stare at the ceiling and await the inevitable calm.

What makes this story even more incredible is that about five years after the invention of 'Killer Dave', he moved jobs to a school twenty miles away from Horbury. On his very first day, he was stopped by a young boy on the corridor, who asked,

'Excuse me, sir. I've heard that you used to be a boxer. Is this true?'

'Yes, but I don't want to talk about it!' snapped Dave and he raised his eyes skywards. Suffice it to say, 'Killer Dave' had no problems at his new school either.

The Educators of Youth

It was in my first year as a teacher that I was fortunate enough to see the Royal Shakespeare Company's ground-breaking adaptation of Charles Dickens' 'Nicholas Nickleby.' Towards the end of the mammoth eight-hour performance, there is a scene played out by two great Dickensian villains, Ralph Nickleby and Wackford Squeers. Squeers is the evil Head Teacher (I've known a few of these in my time) of the wonderfully-named Dotheboys Hall and was played in this production by the rubber-faced Alun Armstrong. He is in prison and, realising that the game is up and his future is unravelling fast, he tells Ralph Nickleby,

'Squeers, noun substantive, a educator of youth. Total, all up with Squeers!' he wails.

There you have it – his whole life and life's work summed up in four words, 'a educator of youth.' He may be one of the most villainous teachers ever invented – perhaps Dickens was pointing out the evils of Yorkshire boarding schools – but in his hour of deepest melancholy and greatest need, he defines himself by his profession. He's also pointing out the most obvious of things, but blissfully ignored by many in the profession – that it's the teacher him/herself that is central to the educational system. You can tinker about with data, methods of teaching and subject content, but the one constant is the 'educator of youth' at the front of the class. It's been the same for centuries, but as time goes by, it never ceases to amaze me how this is so easily and so repeatedly forgotten. It's got so that the hierarchy of an institution (or senior leaders) cannot recognise what a good teacher or a good lesson looks like. The criteria for judgment changes almost daily, is seen by many classroom teachers as 'change for change's sake' and often goes completely against all previously used criteria, which had been valued so highly shortly before. Unsure of how to judge teaching, many schools resort to other means for how to judge staff. You can say what you like, work scrutinies and book checks mean diddly squat. Nobody is going to leave school saying,

'I remember my History lessons. The worksheets were of such high quality and had been trimmed to fit our books. It was lovely to have them marked in non-threatening purple ink (the purple pen of progress) and to be able to respond in green pen.'

When I meet ex-students today, they say things like,

'Do you still tell those jokes about Robert Koch?'

'Do you remember that lesson where we had to do them dodgy dance moves for Egyptian, Greek and Roman medicine?'

Enjoyment and engagement are the keys to success and that's down to the quality of the teacher, not the quality of the exercise book. Teachers are the most important resource in the education system and if we fail to realise and value this, I fear for the future. In my thirty-plus years as a teacher, it has been my pleasure and privilege to work with some extraordinary characters who devoted their time, humour and expertise to become fine examples of 'educators of youth.' 'These are their stories,' as they say in a certain US crime drama.

One of the loudest 'educators of youth' I worked with was a guy we'll call 'Cockney Pete.' Pete was loud, very loud. His idea of a whisper would be like Danny Dyer giving a live commentary from a war zone where everything was 'kicking off.' His language was equally dodgy, especially when he wandered into his extensive knowledge of the Anglo-Saxon vernacular. It was not so much that he'd call 'a spade, a spade', but more of he'd call 'a spade', a 'fackin' spade!' A torrent of abuse was never far from his lips and for some reason, the students came to accept it and embrace it. The school bully hardly flinched when Pete called him 'Fackin' Porky' and, after some objections, his girlfriend with the loose morals even accepted the term 'fat slag.'

On one occasion my friend was teaching a first-year class with some of his own form group mixed in with Cockney Pete's. All of a sudden the calm welcoming environment of his classroom was interrupted by the classroom door bursting open and the invasion of a harassed-looking Pete, who greeted him with,

'Oi, Del! Some bar-stads taxed the bleedin' video again! Any ideas?'

Half of the young students looked on in open-mouthed horror and amazement. The others (from Pete's form) nodded sagely.

On another occasion, a senior member of staff was delivering an assembly about the one-time athlete and M.P., Chris Chataway, who had opened our school hall sometime in the late 1960's. Pete was standing at the back, slowly shaking his head. The eulogy was explaining how and why Sir Christopher had won the first BBC Sports Personality of the Year in 1954, when it was interrupted by an unmistakably loud Cockney voice,

'And a right Tory bar-stad, he was!'

I haven't seen Pete for about thirty years. The last I heard, he'd been appointed as Head Teacher at a large 11-18 school – honestly.

A similar career path was to await another ex-member of staff, who was even crazier that Cockney Pete. Neil, as we'll call him, started off on supply in the PE department and was quickly snaffled to become a permanent member of staff. He was one of the most naturally gifted teachers I've ever worked with in terms of building up great working relationships with all students and (most) staff. He was the life and soul of the classroom, sports pitch and staff room. His rapport with students started when he used to give running commentaries on all football games in PE lessons, a la Brian Glover as Mr Sugden in the film, 'Kes.' Team names were drawn from the upper echelons of European and International football, and even the weakest of footballers was desperate to find out their character in the match. Students hung on his every word and believed him implicitly. When one of his fellow PE teachers was off sick for a few days, he managed to persuade the kids that the guy had been called away to mediate in a dispute in the family business – Thornton's Chocolates.

'Didn't he tell you he was on the board of directors?' he said to the students in all seriousness. 'He's entitled to free samples and is always bringing in boxes and boxes into the staff room. We get so many that we have to throw them away!'

Of course, the students took it in hook, line and sinker and on his return to work, the sick teacher couldn't understand why so many kids were giving him dirty looks, shouting out 'Toffee Man' and asking for free samples.

At one point during renovations to the school site, the staff pigeon holes were moved into the staff room. Neil started to keep a jar of coffee in his and was surprised to notice that the level of coffee in the jar seemed to diminish more quickly than usual. As a result, he installed a curtain rail and curtain across the front of his pigeon hole, so the coffee jar could not be seen. Still the level continued to fall. Further action was necessary and Neil installed a small sensor alarm to the underside of the jar which would trigger off the playing of 'Greensleeves' any time it was disturbed. After much waiting, the alarm sounded one lunch time and one red-faced PE teacher was caught red-handed, reaching through the curtains to access the precious Gold Blend.

Neil also invented a number of staff room games, which have passed into the annals of history, thanks to the removal of a main staff room from most new educational establishments. For a while carpet bowls was a craze, but his best invention was 'staff room cricket', which involved hitting a tennis-ball-sized plastic air-ball with a long cardboard tube. This was usually played only at the end of the school day, when the room was largely empty, apart from staff taking time to relax and up for a quick stress-reducing match. There were clear rules. It was a four if you manged to fire the ball into a side wall, or a six if you reached the back wall, but you could be given out caught, if fielders caught you one-handed after the ball hit the wall or ceiling. The room was full of settees, benches and coffee tables, so fielders either remained seated for safety, or more commonly, risked life and limb by diving across the furniture. A match usually lasted about twenty minutes – until all participants had had at least one innings or until the headmaster came into complain about the noise, as his office was directly below.

Neil's other long-lasting legacy to Horbury was that he was one of the inventors and propagators of the myth that a certain male member of staff, Sandy, wore a wig. This was a legend that was deemed to be for staff consumption only and Neil was so convincing that many gullible teachers believed him immediately and unquestioningly. Every new teacher was told the tale, usually by Neil, but each time he told it, he added a new detail to embellish the story. As a result, in no time at all Sandy came to own not just one wig, but a whole range of them. He kept most of them on a range of mannequin heads in a secret wig room in his house. When Sandy came to school after a weekend haircut, Neil would explain the changed appearance by Sandy's new trial of a Summer/Winter/Leisure/Sporting/Party/Dry Clean only wig, or say that he'd been down to London for a special wig trimming. In another version of the story, Sandy had been a major investor in the wig company which had changed its name to 'Sandy's Syrups' – and in this pre-Internet time, it was not easy to prove Neil a liar. He'd even told one staff member that Sandy was trying out a new 'carpet glue' to replace his usual Velcro, as he had experienced problems with the 'coconut matting lining' in high winds. As a result, on one windy autumnal day, the same member of staff followed Sandy around the school for much of the day, desperately trying to catch a glimpse of the wig base. Imagine our surprise when the teacher swore blind that he'd seen the wig 'nearly fly away.'

After moving on from Horbury, Neil still made guest appearances at staff social events and continued to create havoc. On being introduced to a new French teacher, whose reputation for being exceedingly uninteresting and boorish had preceded him, Neil opened with,

'Ah, you must be Phil. I've heard you're a boring bastard.'

Subtle. At another event he even managed to set fire to a member of staff's trousers. Don't ask. And this man became a Head Teacher.

Another 'character' from the early years was nicknamed 'Billy the Fish' on account of his legendary drinking ability and the fact that he always appeared stone-cold sober (if you ignored the alcohol sweats and prevailing after-shave of cheap lager). On a night out, he'd still be going strong, long after renowned boozers had been poured into taxis or collected by increasingly annoyed partners. When one staff member left him close to midnight, saying that he'd had enough after fourteen pints on the extended 'Westgate Run', Billy snorted,

'Pah! I've spilled more on t' bar towel.'

Rumour had it that Billy brewed forty pints of his own super-strength lager every week in his bath tub. Apparently each batch was ready for consumption every Friday evening, at which point his wife and kids could gain access to the bath tub for their weekly soak. In the meantime Billy would start on the fruits of his labour, which would usually last him until Sunday lunch time, when he could be found down at his local club, sampling a few beers. His drinking was obviously a serious health problem and one which Billy finally admitted to.

One Monday morning, a sober-looking Billy was in the staff room, smoking one of his famous roll-ups. He was slowly shaking his head and not looking his usual cherry-faced cheery self. Steve approached him,

'Are you alright, Billy? You've got a face like a slapped arse.'

'I've been to doctors,' explained Billy.

'Oh, aye?'

'He says I've got to give up these,' he said, stubbing the remains of the thin roll-up in the ash tray, 'and stop drinking alcohol altogether.'

'What're you going to do, Billy?'

'Change me f**kin' doctor!'

Not all teachers are alcoholics – that's a sentence I never thought I would write. Many only drink rarely, but some make up for it when they do. One such is Walt, who still believes to this day that I tried to kill him with booze. We had a bit of a 'leaving do' for a long-serving member of staff on a Thursday night before the final teaching day of the spring term. The night itself – a pub crawl round Ossett – passed off without incident and Walt had sampled a few beers. As he lived in Leeds, he'd arranged to stay at my house in Ossett, so that he didn't have to drive home. When we got home, his problems began. In those days I was into whisky and was building up a reasonable collection of 'drinking whiskies' which, as a generous host, I was eager to share. I took out of the cupboard about eight bottles of Scottish, Irish and even a clear Manx whisky and lined them up on the carpet. It would be rude and too difficult to select one above any other, so we decided to sample a large measure of each one, before continuing on to put an even larger dent into a bottle of Remy Martin cognac. The 'wee small hours' passed by quite comfortably until about 3.45 a.m., when my wife appeared and suggested that we might like to get a few hours' sleep before getting up for school.

That next morning, well three and a half hours later, was horrendous. My head pounded like a jackhammer, my tongue appeared to be adhered to the roof of my mouth and I had serious whisky sweats. If I was bad, 'Whisky Walt' was ten times worse. He looked like a dead man walking. He refused any breakfast on offer but tried to sip some water to take some paracetamol. We somehow managed to get him in the car and I could hear him groaning from the back seat as we headed for school.

'You tried to kill me!' he kept groaning.

A couple of mugs of tea in the staff room seemed to revive me and I was good to go. Walt, however, fared less well and retreated to the gents to throw up. By first lesson, I was back to normal for my third-year History, but Walt's surprise cover lesson for fifth-year Drama was 'interesting.' Directed to the 'Activity Room' to oversee a class preparing for their final examinations, Walt took up a position on top of a six-foot pile of PE exercise mats and, directing the class to 'rehearse', promptly fell asleep. After being woken in time for his own classroom-based lesson later on, he called upon the staff member next-door to 'keep an eye' on his students on two occasions to allow him further 'sick breaks.' The second time he managed to burst a blood vessel in his eye (although when getting it checked out by a doctor the next week, he put it down to a 'violent cough').

By lunch time I was able to put in an appearance at the local pub, as was normal for a Friday at that time. Walt borrowed the office of one of his friends and curled up in a ball on a scrap of carpet in front of an electric fire to continue his slumbers and convalescence. We felt we'd managed to cover up Walt's illness from the hierarchy, until, on my return to school from the pub, I was confronted by an angry senior leader. The lady was known to be a stickler for the rules and would not be able to stop herself from grassing Walt up to the boss.

'I've just seen Walt in Colin's Office. It's a disgrace! He shouldn't be at school,' she insisted.

I thought that I was truly witnessing the end of Walt's glittering career, almost before it began. Somehow I managed to counter with,

'Is he really that bad?'

'He most certainly is,' she insisted. 'He's got that virus that's going around. Of course, I had it much worse than him!'

'I'm sure you did,' I smiled sympathetically.

Within a few days Walt had almost recovered from his 'virus', but it took slightly longer for his bloodshot eye to show no traces of his whisky-induced vomiting. Walt left Horbury for senior management shortly after this, but on the few occasions our paths have crossed, we never fail to laugh about 'the virus.' He still tells everybody who will listen, 'Dave tried to kill me.'

Other colleagues too, went on to reach the dizzy heights (or plumb the lowest depths, depending on your viewpoint) of senior management, having survived similar brushes with alcoholic-inspired illness. Some of them are graduates or seasoned delegates on my one-day CPD training course at Stalyvegas. This involves an early morning meeting in Huddersfield, catching the train to Stalybridge for a couple of hours of serious real ale sampling at the world-famous buffet bar at Stalybridge station, before attending a Stalybridge Celtic football match and participating in a Stalyvegas pub crawl back to the station. Some participants continue to stop for drinks at other stations on their way back to Yorkshire or even opt for clubbing in Wakefield. Most delegates, however, are too 'tired and emotional' and some even end up catching a train in the wrong direction. In the case of one staff member, Rylan, they catch the correct train but end up sleeping through their stop and end up in York.

Rylan appeared to have taken a course in practical joking with the aforementioned fellow PE teacher, Neil. He was always game for a laugh and fortunately, as is essential for all jokers, he could take it as well as dish it out. Rylan only became 'Rylan' when he decided to grow facial hair to improve his boy-band good looks and so naturally came in for a lot of ribbing. The soubriquets 'Grizzly Adams' and 'Papa Smurf' were toyed with, but the teacher's bright white teeth and up-to-date fashion sense meant that 'Rylan' was the obvious winner, especially when some staff called him 'a more effeminate version of Rylan.' Rylan was an expert on the telephone wind-ups and could usually set them up so that people could never think that he was involved.

Rylan was a member of the school's curry club, open only to a select few. On one evening, our expert, Zahid, had organised a visit to a new venue and one which he personally recommended. Unfortunately on the evening itself, Zahid was unable to attend, but we went without him. On arrival there was some confusion about our table and we had to wait about half an hour, but the curry was good and we even sat on a table next to Chris Kamara. After the meal Rylan got us to pose outside the pub next door looking miserable. He then sent it to Zahid, saying that we'd not been allowed into the curry house and had had to go for a drink and a packet of crisps in the pub next door instead. He thought this would wind Zahid up and he'd tell him the truth the next day. When the next day arrived, Zahid found Rylan and told him that he'd already rung up the restaurant to complain and had been promised that the manager would ring him back at 5 pm, when he was expected back. Rylan's face dropped. For once, one of his jolly japes had backfired and he ended up having to ring up the restaurant to apologise for a complete misunderstanding, once he had grovelled to Zahid.

Rylan was much more successful in the winding up of another PE teacher, Tony. Tony is a big supporter of Huddersfield Town and at one home game, in a season a few years back, when the team was struggling and the manager appeared clueless, he'd got out of his seat to ' vent his spleen,' using some very colourful language to reprimand the manager. He was relaying the story in the staff room one Monday morning and Rylan sensed an opportunity. He persuaded one of the ladies on reception to fill in a message sheet which a student delivered to Tony whilst he and Rylan were teaching badminton in the Sports Hall. Right on cue the message was brought in and the student receptionist entered the Sports Hall and searched out Tony. Tony took the note, unfolded it and read something like,

'PC Griffiths from Huddersfield Police is in reception, waiting to speak to you about an incident which happened in the main stand of the Galpharm on Saturday. Please ask Rylan to cover your students.'

Tony's face went white. Perhaps some of those words he'd used on Saturday were a little excessive? Was he going to get charged with a crime? Would he be handcuffed at school? He walked over to Rylan.

'Look after my kids for a minute, I've got a visitor in reception,' he explained.

'Is everything OK?' asked Rylan sweetly, 'you look a little pale.'

'I'll be back in a minute,' and he hurried out.

By the time Tony had aged about ten years and reached reception, another member of staff was waiting for him and explained the entire put-up job.

Rylan's best wind-up involved a new MFL teacher who had been having problems with the payroll at Wakefield MDC, who she believed were under-paying her. She'd contacted them on numerous occasions, had explained her concerns and they'd always promised to call back. This had gone on for a week or so and still the matter had not been resolved. Rylan got one of the reception staff to fill out a 'telephone message form', which was used when the member of staff was teaching or unavailable to take a call. It was brought up to the staff room one lunch time and said something like, 'Don Kiddick from Payroll called to discuss your case. Please call him back on 01924 ****** (the Wakefield MDC Payroll number)'

The member of staff wasted no time in returning the call, making use of the handily-placed staff room phone. Rylan and his co-conspirator sat back in amusement as they witnessed something like,

'Hello. I'd like to speak to Don Kiddick, please.'

(Pause)

'What do you mean?– 'there is no Don Kiddick there.' I got a message from him this morning from this very line!'

(Pause)

'I don't understand. Can you ask around, please? I'm sure somebody must know a Don Kiddick!'

It was only then that the poor girl noticed an almost doubled-up Rylan and his mate laughing like drains that she thought something was a bit strange. She didn't understand why they should have been reduced to gibbering wrecks and only when her friend got her to repeat the name slowly over and over again did she realise the reason for their laughter. Fortunately, Payroll was able to resolve her under-payment issue, although the whereabouts of the elusive Don Kiddick remained a mystery.

Another Stalyvegas graduate who went on to hold the top job at another school was Maths teacher, Marc. He was another fine example of a maverick teacher – always ready to take risks, but one step away from genius and one step away from madness. When unleashed on a strictly traditional Mathematics department at Horbury, he caused havoc, bewilderment and even in some staff, resentment. Some children were now seeing Maths as the highlight of the week, for goodness sake.

On one occasion the Head of Lower School arrived at Marc's classroom to collect a particular student. The girl, Katy, was in a class of thirty that the Head expected to see in the room. Imagine her surprise when, upon entering, only about ten students were seated in the class – the others were nowhere to be seen. The Head looked perplexed and asked if Katy had arrived. She had and Marc informed her that she would be 'in the cupboard.' He knocked on the store room door and shouted,

'Can Katy come out, please?'

The door opened to reveal twenty grinning students and, after a bit of shuffling, pulling and pushing, Katy appeared at the door. Later at the investigation arranged by the Head of Lower School, it emerged that Marc was playing a Maths game and that when a student gave an incorrect answer, they were sent to the 'sin bin' or 'store room'. These were the days before Health and Safety really kicked in and in the end the Head could do little more than tut a bit and move on.

Marc received similar attention for a series of pop posters which started to appear on the walls of his classroom and were regarded by some as 'sexist.' The Deputy Head took particular issue with a certain Spice Girls poster, which was deemed as 'portraying women as sex objects.' I'm sure Marc would disagree and would point out that he customised all of his posters to make a point. The Spice Girls poster was dominated by a large speech bubble coming from Ginger Spice's mouth which was saying, 'I tell you what I want, what I really really want – five A-C at GCSE would be nice.'

He could also point out that his posters tried to level the sexist balance by including a picture of Peter Andre with his top off. Inevitably, he'd added the comment, 'Somebody told Peter that he had a lovely six-pack. Peter wasn't so sure because he'd struggled at GCSE Maths.'

There was always some point behind all of Marc's japes and, as a result, the authorities didn't know how to play him. The students loved his lessons and his jokes; and kids are always impressed with celebrities. It's good to show them a different perspective. Of course, some students are beyond hope. I remember a Year 11 girl (whose career ambition was to be a pole/lap dancer) being obsessed with Madonna and writing in one of her GCSE English assignments,

'I know Madonna has slept around, but if I could achieve what she has achieved, I'd be a sl*g too.'

If Marc could be viewed as a bit of a maverick, Mad Mick was as mad as a box of frogs. I recall one night before a school student-teacher drama production, some of the staff members of the cast had come to my home for something to eat. On entering the house, Mick announced that he needed to have a lie-down for an hour, or he'd be unable to perform that night. I pointed him in the direction of the spare bedroom and forgot all about him as I set about preparing the food. Thirty minutes later, after my wife had returned from her work, she came running down the stairs to inform me that there was a 'strange man' under the covers in our bed, with his clothes strewn all over the bedroom. That'll be Mick, then.

When the industrial action was on in the 1980's, teachers were instructed by the union to leave the school site every lunch time. About a dozen of us walked down the road to a nearby pub. We usually had a soup or a sandwich, but Mad Mick wangled it so that he could order from the children's menu. Accordingly, for every day for the best part of a year, Mick would tuck into a meal of two fish fingers, chips and beans, washed down with a glass of orange squash – every day was the same. Some staff (including Mick) continued this practice even after the action ended, but most of us stopped going when a member of the pub staff, in all seriousness, complained that she was fed up having to hoover up the crumbs we left every day. Mick however, continued on his diet of fish fingers until the day he left Horbury. In this age of almost daily pub closures, I'm sure there are lots of publicans who would gladly run the vacuum cleaner round if they were guaranteed a regular daily clientele of an extra twelve or so, putting a few quid into the till.

Mad Mick's eccentricity continued until the day he left. Announcing that he would be too self-conscious to deliver a speech, Mick recorded one on the school's only video camera. When it came time to deliver his speech, he promptly pressed the play button and settled down to watch his own performance (which included a declaration of love for another teacher), without a hint of self-conscience.

Of course many of the students were as eccentric as the staff. 'Rob' was one of the nicest kids I've ever taught. He was registered as SEN but never ceased to entertain and win over people with his affability, humour and candour. As soon as he arrived at Horbury, he took it upon himself to learn as many names of the staff as he could and would always seek to engage you in conversation. One night, on 'Bus Duty', he was his usual cheery self.

'Good afternoon, Mr Matthews. How are you?'

'I'm fine, Rob. Have you had a good day?'

'Yes, fine thanks. What are you having for your tea tonight?'

At this point another member of staff, a short and round lady, approached and caught Rob's puzzled gaze. He had never met her before and so all enquiries about that night's cuisine came to an abrupt halt when he addressed her with,

'Hello, I don't think I know you, do I? I'm Rob.'

'Hello, Rob. I'm Mrs Trent.'

Rob look slightly puzzled, but replied quickly with,

'There's a word for people like you.'

'Is there? What's that?'

'Dwarves!'

'That's nice!'

It wasn't the only time that Rob's straight talking caused embarrassment. I recall waiting on-board a North Sea ferry after a weekend at the German Christmas markets. The place was heaving with people listening intently to the intercom, waiting to be called for disembarkation, when the silence was broken by Rob shouting,

'And who did you sleep with last night, Mr Matthews?'

This was mild compared to some of the graffiti which could appear around the school at a moment's notice. One of my responsibilities in days-gone-by was to organise the running of the school examinations – a sort of assistant to the examinations secretary. The worst part of this was the setting up of the examination room in the school gymnasium. This entailed laying a jigsaw of massive filthy plastic sheeting all over the gym floor to protect it from the chairs and desks that were going to be brought in. Much of the sheeting was years old and reeked of ancient cheesy feet. It also had large gaping holes which had to be patched up with newer, smaller lengths of sheeting. Once it had been taped down, the desks and chairs would be ferried in by students (Health and Safety might have a few issues with this today) from the store in the basement of the music block at the other side of the school. This basement (an abandoned toilet block) housed close to two hundred wooden desks piled up on top of each other and enormous stacks of wooden chairs, some of them stored in the actual toilet cubicles. It had to be tackled carefully. It was back-breaking work and had to be done again in reverse at the end of the exam period. The only good thing about doing this task was that you could read again some of the graffiti that earlier scholars had left for posterity. Some of the desks were greeted like old friends, when you read messages such as, 'Dunlop blows goats – I have proof', 'Stevens has got breath like a camel's arse' and the all-time classic, 'Tina Short has swallowed more semen than the Bermuda Triangle.'

Whilst on the subject of graffiti, the largest-ever graffiti I've ever seen at school greeted me one Monday morning in my third year of teaching. I'd been allocated a portakabin classroom, gloriously numbered 'Room 101' (pretty close to what George Orwell had in mind in '1984', I think) which was sited as far away as possible from anyone else, next to the long jump pit. As I approached the room from underneath the junior block, I could not fail to see on the large gable-end, a large bell-end. A massive erect phallus was being 'pleasured' by a small hand. In large letters the artist had added the caption, 'Jackson wanking Matthews'. I felt a mixture of shock and outrage, but also was secretly pleased that I had obviously been deemed important enough to lampoon. The owner of the 'hand' however, a senior leader, certainly felt the first two emotions and saw to it that the evidence was removed by the caretaking staff before any students arrived, although for many years after a shower of rain, I'm pretty sure that the outline of the phallus could still be seen, if you looked from a certain angle.

Somme Stories

If schooldays are supposed to be the happiest days of your life, for many students school trips are amongst the happiest of their memories from their days at school. Over the years I've been on many trips both home and abroad and most of them were before the unhealthy obsession with Health and Safety which has sought to increase stress, red tape and reams of paperwork for teachers. Today, in order to take a trip across the road to the local park, after gaining formal permission from the 'Events Team', you have to fill in forms to explain how you would cross the road – maybe at the pelican crossing outside the school gate? – and how you would react to cases of sunstroke, hypothermia and an attack of killer bees. For me the final straw came a few years back when I was organising a joint Humanities project with another local school. To be able to take ten of our students on a minibus taxi and then to walk from a local castle to a café, after completing all the necessary paperwork, I was required to undergo an interrogation by the governors of the school. They noticed that the route to the café was on a footpath which came within thirty metres of a lake and as a result, considered this to be hazardous. I explained that we were not canoeing, surfing or white water rafting, but one governor thought that it would be a good idea to coil a large length of 'sturdy rope' around my waist, just in case. Suffice it to say, I did not take the rope and retired from trip participation at this time.

To show how much Health and Safety has changed over time – some twenty-odd years earlier, my mate Richard had taken a group of six 'bad lads' by himself on a weekend of outdoor pursuits, staying in an authority-owned hostel deep in the Yorkshire Dales. They were miles from anywhere, had no mobile phones and anything could have happened. Richard had not filled in any forms and amazingly nobody got sunstroke or hypothermia or were bothered by the killer bees. The lads, so unused to being treated so well or leaving their estate in Leeds, had behaved impeccably until the journey home. Late one Sunday afternoon, as Richard drove the minibus home, two of the lads on the back seat, started a fight. The others urged them to stop and not spoil their chance of a future visit, but in the ensuing melee, a side window popped out and smashed onto the road. As Richard stopped the bus, the back door flew open and one of the fighters ran off into the distance towards a nearby village. The remaining five boys were keen to tell Richard that it wasn't his fault and the six of them marched towards the nearby village on foot. They arrived minutes later and there was nobody to be seen. The lads started shouting the boxer's name. At that point an old man appeared from a barn and addressed Richard,

'Have you lost summat?'

'I don't suppose you've seen a lad about 15?'

'Come with me! I thought somebody would be up for him. I saw him snooping around and thought he was a bit dodgy.'

Richard and the five lads were shown to a nearby barn and upon entering saw the boxer tied to an old wooden chair in the middle - now that's how to use a length of 'sturdy rope.' Richard untied his student and after declining the offer of the rope to tie the boxer up in the minibus on the way home, they returned to the bus and Leeds. The 'accidental damage' to the bus was repaired and the incident was never mentioned again. In today's litigious society, I'm sure the farmer would have been sued for compensation or even imprisoned, but in the 1980's he was simply seen as a 'good citizen' helping out a respected teacher.

If Health and Safety was slack in England in the 1980's, abroad it was almost non-existent. I recall making two trips to northern Spain where there were much more serious dangers. We stayed in a lovely hotel on the beach at Isla, near Santander. On our first visit, after a twenty–four hour coach journey, the coach took a wrong turn about five miles from the hotel and got stuck on a beach. We all had to get out to push to get it back onto the road. On arrival at the hotel, the kids rushed to put on costumes to swim in the sea. Most of the staff watched from a safe distance – it was only that evening that we were warned about the areas of quicksand, dangerous currents and sudden storms. Indeed, we witnessed a freak high tide when we were there on our second visit and one unfortunate Fiat owner saw their precious car being taken out to sea from the nearby headland.

Other 'horror stories' could have resulted from our visits to a decaying fairground with a rickety wooden rollercoaster and a sea trip on an open vessel from Santander with seemingly no hand-rails, lifejackets or emergency precautions. As a non-swimmer, I felt particularly anxious and wished I'd stayed on land with the only non-participant from our party, a fellow teacher. This guy had overdone it the night before and was a strange green colour even before mention of a boat trip. The party had been served egg and chips for tea the previous evening and as a number of students didn't fancy the egg part of the meal, the teacher had added them to his plate. He must have had about a dozen eggs – Big Ian would have seen it as a starter – and then washed it down with about four pints of San Miguel. The teacher decided to have a lie-down on a harbour-side bench whilst we tackled the ocean waves. We returned an hour later to find him surrounded by Spanish police, who were about to make an arrest. Apparently he had fallen asleep and given his inability to produce any documents (his passport was locked away in the hotel safe), or be able to speak any Spanish, they took one look at his sickly, unshaven appearance and had decided he must be an illegal immigrant or a vagrant. Fortunately the Spanish teacher was able to explain the misunderstanding and the police were on their way.

We saw the same police later in the week when we called them to the hotel. The students had been given an hour's free time to go shopping in Santander and on their return one student reported that some boys had bought some dodgy gear. When we arrived back at the hotel, we got the students to show us their purchases and uncovered a handful of school-banned lighters, a large number of evil-looking knives and even a bullwhip. It was the knives that were the scariest item – they included some flick knives and even a couple of specialised hunting knives that could skin a crocodile. The police were called and told us that only the flick-knives were illegal. They took them away with them and were delighted that our students knew the names of the shops where they had bought them. The evil hunting knives were kept by the staff for the holiday and handed over to the parents on our return. One parent was delighted with his knife as he was a keen hunter, but most just shook their heads in disbelief – 'What on earth possessed you to buy a thing like this?' The most embarrassment however, was shown by a red-faced mother who took delivery of her son's bullwhip.

My most vivid memories of school trips though are linked to one of the most important traditions of the History department in the old school – the annual trip for the students to the WW1 battlefields of the Somme and Ypres. Steve, my ex-Head of Department, was an expert in anything to do with the First World War and his ability to relate the modern-day landscape to that in 1916 never ceased to amaze me. He led a series of annual trips which to many students became one of the most important and poignant parts of their education. I still get students today reminiscing about the visits and some still have the diaries they completed whilst on the trip. The trips were always jam-packed with visits to memorials, cemeteries and museums and usually ended with attendance at the emotional nightly remembrance service at the Menin Gate in Ypres.

Each year travel companies would vie for our custom and we would experience a range of central bases and accommodation options. On one occasion we found ourselves arriving early in the evening at a hotel in the centre of Arras, only to be told we had a two-and-a-half mile walk (as the coach driver was 'out of hours') to the dining place at a dodgy café on some industrial estate – apparently the travel company discovered that a meal there worked out a few francs a head cheaper than the hotel's own restaurant in the building next door. Another time we arrived at a 'Campanile' to find that half the rooms were 'doubles', rather than 'twins' as promised. As a result many of the students and all of the staff were forced to share a bed. Most of the girls were fine about this, although some of the lads 'kicked off' until we reminded them about the young soldiers their age sleeping in the dug-outs in the trenches with rats and lice etc. When it came time to retire, Steve and I sat up in our bed for a while sharing a bottle of wine and reading up for the next day – we felt and looked like Morecambe and Wise.

The most memorable venue, however, was a small village hotel near Lens, which we returned to visit on a number of occasions. The hotel was run by a seventy year old Yorkshireman called 'Johnny' who had liberated the town at the end of World War 2. According to him, he had liberated half of the women as well and with such generous hospitality, he had decided to stay. He married a local girl and started his thriving hotel and restaurant business.

The first time we visited the hotel we did not know that the owner spoke English. Steve (who had taken 'A' level French) decided that yours truly (complete with a dodgy 'C' grade at 'O' level) should do all the talking. As we entered the building, I began with,

'Bonjour. Nous avons un reservation. Nous sommes les professeurs et les eleves de Horbury School en Wakefield'

'I knew you'd be from some bloody field,' countered Johnny. 'Tha's left door open! Put wood in th'ole!'

In the first few years of our visits, Johnny was very keen to impress and would often top up your drink, urging you to 'get it down yer neck.' He served up eggs, burgers and even fish fingers (Mad Mick would have been impressed) with chips for the kids, but presented a partial French menu for the staff. I say 'partial' because I remember one night being served foie-gras, fish soup, egg and chips, a dessert and cheeseboard! One year he was extremely unimpressed when he discovered that one female member of staff was a vegetarian. She was given a cheese salad each night and Johnny told us, 'No wonder her hair's a bloody mess - she needs to eat meat!'

Johnny also had a scrawny-looking parrot which originally belonged to his mother-in-law and was kept in its cage in the main bar (the parrot, not the mother-in-law). The bird had picked up on Johnny's loud voice and frequently told customers to 'Bugger off!', 'Put wood in th'ole,' or 'Get it down yer neck, yer French bastard!' One night, as Johnny was doing his best silver service with the cheeseboard, Steve pointed to a blue cheese and asked if it was 'blue brie.' As quick as a flash, Johnny had countered with,

'Oh, bloody hell! Parrot's shat on cheeseboard again!'

On the last morning of our first visit to Johnny's, we were finishing up our breakfast coffee when Johnny appeared and asked what time we were planning to leave. When we told him that the cases were already on the coach and we were hoping to leave within the next ten minutes, I've never seen a man move so fast. In what seemed like seconds staff appeared from all directions and transformed the main bar area into Johnny's Duty Free Paradise. He was offering packs of beer and cases of his excellent house wine at 'special prices' for staff and had brought in some really dodgy-looking (and smelling) perfumes, after-shaves and cosmetic kits for the kids to inflict on their parents. The kids were 'mad for it' and he shifted loads of the dodgy gear, but when Steve declined the bargain offer for a case of Kronenbourg 1664, he was told in no uncertain terms –

'Bugger off t'Hypermarket then! Get ripped off, tosser!'

He did and he was.

By the time of our third (and what turned out to be our last) annual visit, things had taken a massive turn for the worse. Johnny had been taken ill and was only a pale shadow of his former self. He had been ordered by his doctor to take a back seat and his empire was now being run by one of his sons, Jean. The biggest change was that the small night club at the back of the hotel, which had been used in previous years by the kids for a disco on the last night, had been replaced by a brothel. Jean told staff that as residents, we would be entitled to a hefty discount and even offered one teacher the special deal of a full refund and a bottle of champagne prize if he could 'last all night' with the top prostitute. Suffice it to say, we declined his offer and wondered about trying to find another hotel, but as we were a party of fifty plus in the middle of nowhere, we had no option but to stay in the hotel and keep the students completely unaware of the knocking shop.

The other change we noticed was that at about 9.30p.m. each evening, another coach party arrived for a 'late supper' and all-inclusive drinking, before being poured back onto their coach at midnight for the final journey to their own hotel about ten miles away. Needless to say, it was unbelievably noisy and trying to get our students to get to bed at 10.30p.m. and asleep was an impossibility. On one particular evening we noticed that the visitors' coach driver, a large and very vocal Scouser, was really knocking back the free alcohol. There was absolutely no way he would be able to drive the bus and this was confirmed a few minutes later when he fell off his bar stool and then proceeded to pick a fight with Jean. He swung (and missed) with a massive right hander before landing a short left into Jean's face. The next thing you know, Jean had smashed a bottle of red wine on the counter and was about to 'bottle' the driver. (I could imagine what Johnny would have said, 'What are you doing smashing the decent red? Use the white, tosser!'). Three of our staff jumped into action – one of us managed to wrestle the broken bottle from Jean's grasp, whilst the other two pinned him to the bar.

'Leave it,' I shouted, 'he's not worth it!'

'You'll get yourself in trouble,' warned Al, 'the police will lock you up.'

'I own the police!' snarled Jean.

We managed to carry the drunken coach driver outside and in the end our own driver came to the rescue, taking the drunk and all his all-inclusive customers back to their hotel in our coach.

The next morning, a massively hung-over Scouser was back at our hotel to pick up his coach. He actually had the nerve to pop in for a coffee before his departure. As he thanked our driver for his help and us for saving him from disfigurement, a bristling Jean appeared, dabbing his swollen nose and black eye with a cloth from an ice bucket. He turned to the coach driver and slowly and calmly he said,

'If you ever show your face here again, you're dead. I'll kill you. You'll never be seen again. I own the police.'

He then turned his attention to us.

'You should not have got involved. It was after ten o'clock and you should all be asleep. When you come next year, you will be in bed by ten.'

On the final day of this trip, once all the bags and students were safely on the coach, Steve popped back into the bar to tell Jean what he really thought about the 'changes' and the new regime. Jean didn't seem to take him too seriously.

'I'll see you next year – you've already booked.'

'We've not booked and I can guarantee we'll never ever step inside your hotel again!' replied Steve; and he was absolutely right.

On another occasion we were unfortunate enough to stay in a dreadful youth hostel/activity centre, hidden in the Belgian countryside near Diksmuide. The food was shockingly bad and as we queued up for our nightly slop, our lippy coach driver announced in a voice for all the party to hear, 'I'm not eating this f**king shite!' He stormed out of the building, got into his coach and disappeared into the night, searching for steak and chips.

The only good thing about the hostel was the bar/recreation area. One side dispensed alcoholic drinks for the teachers and sixth-form visitors whilst the other was more of a youth club with pool tables, gaming machines and a smaller soft drinks bar for most students. One evening, as the staff sipped a well-deserved beer after a long day on the battlefields, a lad from my form approached and in a low voice, said,

'Sir, you need to come and see this – now.'

Steve and I followed him into the other side of the bar, just in time for us to witness the Head Girl accepting the delivery of two halves of lager. We rounded up all of our students, alerted the remaining staff and commandeered one of the classrooms on the floor above for an impromptu meeting.

You could cut the silence with a knife. The students looked down on the floor, waiting for the inevitable telling off. They didn't have to wait long. Steve started by saying how he wasn't angry, 'just disappointed' as he felt 'let down' (an all-time classic). I steamed in with how Steve had left his young family at home to give up his holiday to spend with them – and this is how they repaid him. Allan added how the young soldiers of World War One didn't have the opportunity to drink alcohol – the behaviour of the students sullied the sacrifice the brave lads had made. Alicia ended the tirade by wondering what their parents and the Head Teacher would think of such behaviour.

The students were all ashen-faced and some had started to sob quietly. Steve asked all those who had sampled the alcohol to raise a hand and to our surprise, about fifteen did (although we later found out that they shared four halves of lager between the fifteen). We made a note of their names and Steve said,

'Right, get to your rooms and get some sleep. We're up at 7.30 tomorrow and I don't want to hear a peep from anyone until then. Now get out.'

The students shuffled off slowly, even some of the innocent ones were crying and some of the guilty were apologising profusely. One boy remained standing by his chair, shaking and swaying and seemingly unable to move. Roger, a school governor who had accompanied us on the trip, approached him sympathetically, asking

'Are you alright, son? Did you drink too much?'

'No it's not that. It's just that I've just never been so scared in all my life!'

Roger helped him to his room and the lad recovered – I saw him about five years later, pulling pints in a pub in Horbury, so obviously he wasn't scarred for life. In hindsight, perhaps we were a bit OTT with the telling off, but we had a governor present and needed to show that we were doing everything above board.

We gave the students about half an hour to settle down and then began our nightly ritual of patrolling the corridors to ensure all was quiet and nobody was 'sleepwalking'. To nobody's surprise, peace and quiet reigned, but then, just as we were about to head for our own beds, we were alerted to the sound of raised voices. It was coming from the room of a group of four, usually quiet and well-behaved Year 11 girls. Steve and I listened in.

'You're a lying bitch! Why should we get done and you don't? You should have owned up like the rest of us. I'm gonna tell Sir and you'll be in deep shit!'

Steve and I looked at each other in amazement and he rapped on the door, asking for the girls to open up. A red-faced and very angry tall girl opened the door and faced him.

'What's all this noise about, Kim? Whatever's the matter?' asked Steve.

'It's Lisa, sir. She's a lying cow. She had alcohol like the rest of us, but she didn't own up, so her name's not on the list.'

I looked past Kim into the room and spied Lisa, a five foot nothing, straight 'A' student from my own form and one of my favourites. I called her to the door. Her eyes were redder than Whisky Walt's bad eye and tears were streaming down her face.

'Is this true, Lisa?' I asked gently.

'I didn't . . . want to . . . but they made me try it. . . I didn't like it. . . so I spat it out!' stammered Lisa, shaking as she delivered her defence.

I was unable to speak, as I could feel tears welling up in my own eyes, but fortunately I was saved by Steve who brought proceedings to an end by calmly announcing,

'Just try and get some sleep. We're not having an inquest over this now. We'll talk in the morning.'

The next morning the cloud of gloom was raised when Steve announced that he wasn't going to let one mistake ruin a great trip. He promised that nothing more would be said about the matter and he would rip up the list of names, much to the appreciation of the 'Horbury 15' and Lisa.

On another occasion we were joined on our Somme trip by some staff and students from another school. Some of their students were a bit more 'streetwise' than their Horbury counterparts and we knew we'd have to be on the lookout for attempts to get alcohol. We were staying in a small village hotel and fortunately there were only two outlets open for alcohol in the times we were there. In those days, it was seen as fine to allow the students an hour of 'free time' after the evening meal and a chance to 'stretch their legs.' Accordingly, two staff stayed at the hotel to monitor bar sales there and the others discretely followed the students around the village and hid in the back room of the other hostelry. Undetected they watched all the Horbury students order an array of soft drinks, hot chocolate and crisps. It was only when the tallest of the non-Horbury students got to the bar that anything out of the ordinary happened. This lad looked about fifteen going on twenty-five, sported a fine display of designer stubble and spoke in a low voice,

'Two cokes, please – oh, and a large beer.'

The bar owner was just passing him the beer when his History teacher appeared at his shoulder. Without blinking, the lad smiled and said,

'There you go, sir. I thought you might appreciate a beer. Cheers!' and he raised a glass of coke. Very cool.

Less cool were some of the staff who got to go on the trip. One History teacher went missing after an evening meal and could not be found. We'd hammered on her bedroom door, scoured the streets of the village and questioned all the students. We were about to phone the police, when the hotel owner lent us a master key, so we could check her room, just in case. One of the female staff volunteered to do the check and found the woman fully clothed, listening to her headphones whilst lying on the bed. Apparently, she felt a bit tired and decided to have an early night, without bothering to tell anybody or worry about her responsibilities to the students. It came as no surprise when she phoned in sick at the start of the school's HMI inspection and did not re-appear until a week later when it was all over.

The least cool event happened on the final morning of one trip. As the coach neared the final stop in France, the large Auchan hypermarket in Calais, a member of staff appeared at Steve's shoulder and whispered,

'Steve, I've shit myself!'

'You dirty bastard!' replied Steve jokingly.

'No, I really have.'

Fortunately the coach was pulling into the large car park of the hypermarket and whilst the students spent the last of their French francs on French breads, chocolate and coke and the majority of staff loaded up on duty free, one teacher bought himself a new pair of jeans and undercrackers, before cleaning himself up in the public toilets. He deposited his soiled clothing in a waste bin near the coach before re-boarding. As the coach pulled out of the car park, a French tramp could be seen rummaging through the waste bin. A look of abject horror told everyone that he had uncovered a ghastly surprise.

Usually on these trips we took a languages teacher to speak French for us, but occasionally we had to struggle to fend for ourselves. At one venue, where the staff spoke 'little English', I had to explain that one of our young girls had recently dislocated her jaw and was unable to chew. She had to take drinks through a straw and could just about manage to feed herself a spoonful of soup or yogurt. As I didn't know the French for 'dislocated jaw' and many other key terms, I tried to convey meaning through actions and simplified words. The receptionist looked on in horror and revealed the weakness of my charade when she said,

'You mean – she has no mouth!'

I felt much more confident when we arrived in Ostend for a couple of nights in a two-centre holiday after our first two days in Arras. That night I used some well-rehearsed French phrases to order drinks for the staff, only to be told,

'Please don't speak French. We do not like it.'

Some of the strangest characters we met on these trips were the museum owners. There must be a training school somewhere that teaches them how to be eccentric, strange or completely mad. The most normal of all the owners we encountered built a trench museum in his back garden and ran a really good café as well. He also carried a range of souvenirs which were of varied quality.

I particularly remember buying a T-shirt emblazoned with a picture of one of my favourite WW1 heroes, Barney Hines and the slogan 'Lest we forget.' It was only when I got this 1 euro bargain home that I noticed the spelling mistake 'Let's we forget', which kind of reverses the meaning of the adage. Even so, I can still treasure the shirt for the photograph of Barney.

Allow me to tell you about him. John 'Barney' Hines was born in Liverpool in 1873 and after failing to join the army at the age of fourteen, embarked on a series of adventures before ending up in Australia. He claimed to be 28 (actually 42) when he enlisted in the Australian army and was sent to Europe to fight. He gained a reputation for bravery and 'souvenir hunting' and after a picture of him with some of his 'German souvenirs' appeared in a newspaper, he came to the attention of the Kaiser who wanted him dead or alive. He favoured using Mills bombs (hand grenades) and a machine gun ('to hose the bastards down'), rather than the service rifle and he once captured a German pillbox containing sixty-three soldiers single-handedly. Reputed to have killed more soldiers than any other Australian in WW1, he was badly injured by shell-fire and hit again when his hospital was bombed, but he carried out and dragged others to safety whilst on crutches himself. Some of his crazier souvenirs included a piano, a grandfather clock and a couple of suitcases full of banknotes which he had liberated from the cellars of a bank which had been bombed. He even tried to re-enlist for WW2 at the ripe old age of 66, but was turned down – although he did manage to stow away in a lifeboat on a troop ship, which had to return to port to repatriate its unwanted cargo. He never received much commendation in his lifetime and died poor and alone in 1958. RIP Barney – rebel, hero and legend.

One of the strangest museum's we discovered was a reconstructed trench museum deep in   the middle of nowhere-in-particular in Belgium. Unfortunately it was pulled down and destroyed a few years after the death of the owner. It was barely standing when we first visited it and a few years later it was boarded up and overgrown. The owner was an old guy who lived on site. He had created a trench museum with thousands of shells, uncovered a German mineshaft to some underground tunnels and even built a pool which at one point he'd tried to run as a sort of pleasure boating lake. The guy had a bedroom/kitchen/living room which opened out directly onto the museum. It had probably been decorated in the 1930's and was adorned with half-empty tins, heaps of fading newspapers and piles of unwashed dishes, which didn't seem to change from year to year. The most disturbing feature was the small bed by the window covered by a grey sheet pulled back to reveal a bare mattress and a sleeve-less pillow stained with the greasy imprint of the old man's head. To be fair, he always welcomed visitors and was immensely proud of his two favourite possessions, a small cannon (which he was keen to fire as a coach party was about to leave) and a framed photograph of him shaking the hand of Adolf Hitler (apparently Adolf had been stationed near there during WW1 and had returned for a visit in WW2).

If this guy was a bit strange, he had nothing on the owner of another trench museum nearer to Ypres, whom we nicknamed 'The Belgian Tommy Cooper.' Tommy must have been at least six-feet-four and when he spoke he did actually sound like Tommy Cooper. If you can imagine Tommy Cooper actually speaking the following lines with a slight Belgian twang, it would be like you were actually there.

'It's good to see you again – a drink for the professeurs!' would be his standard opening line and within seconds one of his assistants would conjure up a couple of beers.

He would ask how many students were with us before making up his own charges – some years were much cheaper than others - and he always substantially undercut the advertised prices for 'regulars.'

'Today the admission price is twenty French francs or eighty Belgian francs, but for you, I give you the special rate. Fifteen French francs or sixty Belgian francs for students and free for the professeurs. More drinks for the professeurs!'

More drinks would appear before we'd even sipped the first beers and Steve would start to count out the entry fee from a wad of notes, pausing every now and then to take a drink, but Tommy always kept his eyes on the money and never lost count. By the time I'd get back with the students from the coach, Steve would be on his third round of drinks and Tommy would be all smiles as he counted in the students to check we hadn't pulled a fast one.

The museum itself was amazing. It had original and reconstructed trenches and tunnels and was usually deep in a muddy sludge – one year it was so thick that a couple of students had to be hauled out, losing their wellington boots in the process and covering themselves from head to toe in mud. It was even rumoured that Tommy emptied his toilet into the trench and often the stench seemed to support that theory. Sometimes the route of the trenches changed from year to year and we were sure he'd dug some new ones. The museum also had an excellent collection of 3D photographs viewed through a number of ancient wooden stereoscopes laid out in a room, full of unique WW1 artefacts.

One of the strangest things about Tommy was his feet. Yes, they were enormous like him, and apparently he struggled to find comfortable shoes to fit them. As a result, he tended to walk around the museum barefoot, displaying a cornucopia of black, cheese-infested nails, hammer toes and bunions.

One year we entered the museum for the usual 'Drinks for the professeurs!' rigmarole and I subtly checked out his feet – same as ever, no shoes or socks. I returned to the coach and at the end of my short introduction to the museum over the coach microphone, I warned the students about Tommy's feet.

'This is one of the very best museums on the Western Front, but the owner is very sensitive about his feet. Under no circumstances should you try to sneak a peek at them. Please be sensitive. Remember, don't look at his feet.'

Of course, if you tell the kids not to do something, they really struggle not to do it. The way into the museum was through a sort of turnstile, which Tommy operated from behind a low counter. I stood back and watched the students enter. I counted no fewer than nineteen students who peered over the counter in an attempt to spy Tommy's feet – one small girl even hauled herself up onto the counter to get a better view. Some of these children will have been emotionally damaged for life – but you can't say I didn't warn them. No Health and Safety issues to report here.

Health and Safety was a major concern on these trips, however. Students were always closely supervised at all sites – they had been warned about the French student who had blown himself up by walking through an uncleared area near Vimy Ridge or the French farmer whose tractor had fallen into a large undiscovered WW1 tunnel when ploughing the fields near Thiepval. It never ceased to amaze me when we used to do 'police searches' in the fields around La Boiselle or the Triple Tambour mines, the sheer volume of debris we'd find from a conflict some eighty years earlier. Farmers left freshly discovered unexploded shells by the side of their fields for the bomb disposal people and we always found pieces of shell, bullets, belt buckles, barbed wire or sometimes bones. Some museums even sold pieces of debris as souvenirs – I once bought a well-preserved outer casing of a Mill's bomb from Tommy. One year though, an over-zealous customs official at Dover called in the bomb squad and forced us to wait for two-and-a-half hours whilst they searched the coach for 'live material.' Of course, there was none.

Years later a new Head Teacher questioned the safety of many of the pieces we had in the History department 'museum' to help us with our studies on WW1. She could not see the need for rusty, blunt scraps of barbed wire (which she somehow thought could injure students) or empty shell or bullet casings. She even suggested that the remains of a WW1 French rifle (without even a firing mechanism) could be used by a teacher to put the lives of students at risk. Steve was forced to dismantle the museum and such bad feeling sadly caused the Somme trips to pass into history.

The Sporting Life

As a massive spectator sports fan, it's always been the biggest regret in my life that I have never been any good at any sport I've actually tried to play. At school I'd failed or been rejected at most sports, but when I started teaching at Horbury, the age range of players in staff sporting activities, from their early twenties to their early sixties, meant that I had more of a chance of at least getting a game. Friday nights used to be 'Sports Night' and five (or more) a side football, cricket, basketball, volleyball and badminton were all tried, but 'short tennis' was the game preferred by most.

To the uninitiated, it was played on a badminton court with the net set up like a tennis match. Competitors had an old wooden bat and whacked a plastic air ball back and forth across the net. Overhead serving was not allowed, but the scoring and everything else was just like lawn tennis. We usually played doubles, could set up some fearsome rallies and frequently had to stop for broken balls. Whisky Walt and his doppelganger mate were probably the Number 1 seeds and were nicknamed 'The Dangerous Brothers.' We even tried to organise short tennis matches against other schools, but it turned out that nobody else liked the game as much as us.

Football was more successful with games against other schools and for a while we even had a joint weekly five-a-side with staff from two other schools as well. It all stopped though when one of the opposition took exception to an allegedly heavy tackle and punched the tackler in the face. Subtle, unnecessary and '#awks' as the kids today would say. Eleven-a-side matches were much more difficult to organise and many staff were less than keen, especially after a History teacher suffered a serious leg-break in a staff/student match. Sometimes sides had to be filled with a number of 'ringers' to make up the numbers, or more likely, improve the odds of winning. I remember one school fielding three pacy eighteen-year-old students to bolster their side. Amazingly when we played them, we took a six-nil lead by half-time with our centre-forward (a regular supply teacher at the school) scoring all six of our goals. He was rested for the second half to give our opponents a chance and was replaced by me. I think we eventually won 7-2, with me touching the ball twice. In spite of this, when it came to getting a re-match, we failed to raise a team.

Cricket was a different story. You could always guarantee to get eleven lads interested, especially if there was the suggestion of a beer or two at close of play. We always liked to play twenty overs per side and everybody (apart from the wicketkeeper) got to bowl two overs. Batsmen had to retire at the end of an over, if they had made 25 or more, but could bat again at the end of the innings, if required.

My first ever match for the Horbury staff team was an away fixture in the glorious surroundings of Ermystead's School in Skipton. You changed in the pavilion at the top of a hill and walked down a set of steps and through a wicker gate onto the square below. It was like walking out to bat at Lord's. As the new boy, it was decided that I should open the batting with Al, an experienced cricketer and all-round sportsman.

We ran down the pavilion steps onto the square to a smattering of polite applause. Al took the strike and the bowler delivered a wild, wide full-toss, way down the leg-side. Al (a left-hander, like me) got a bat on it and it sailed to the boundary for four runs. The second ball was an exact replica of the first, but this time Al failed to make contact and as it zipped past the wicketkeeper, we sauntered through for a bye.

I was now on strike and was ready for it. This was my chance to make a name for myself and with such rank bowling, even I'd bag a few runs. Anything down the leg-side is meat and drink to a left hander and as I went to sweep the ball high over square-leg, I witnessed the perfect yorker-length ball uproot the leg stump. I padded glumly back to the long walk up to the steps up to the pavilion. It was difficult to discern which of my colleagues were engaged in a slow ironic applause and which were overcome with unbridled laughter.

I never did have the best of luck at Skipton. Years later, I was asked to open the batting again and had made about seventeen runs, when I was given out lbw by a stand-in umpire. The regular umpire had absented himself for an over or two for a call of nature and had managed to borrow one of the Y10 students from the crowd to stand in for him. As we didn't usually play the lbw rule at staff games and I was about half-way down the track trying to hoist a spinner out of the ground, I was less than impressed to see the chubby finger of Tetley Minor go up in response to a strangled appeal from his Maths teacher.

Skipton was also the first time we played against a woman in the opposition XI. When the young lady came into bat, our skipper went over to the fast bowler and urged him to 'take it easy.' After dispatching his next two balls to the boundary with glorious cover drives, the bowler was heard to mutter 'she can f**k right off!' Accordingly the next ball was a ripper – short and fast. The batsman just rocked back on her feet and hooked him for six out of the ground. We later heard that she played for Yorkshire Ladies and in a previous staff game had hit the ball so far and hard that it had smashed a window in the canteen, about a hundred metres away at the bottom of the hill.

The funniest incident at Skipton though concerned Hugh, a forty-something Technology teacher. We had batted first and were now defending a smallish total. Hugh was stationed on the boundary and when the batsman hammered a cover drive vaguely in his direction, we shouted at him to run and stop the ball. He started to sprint along the boundary line, but it seemed clear that he would not be able to get there in time – until he stuck out a hopeful leg. The ball thudded into his ankle and Hugh started to jump up and down, screaming in pain and clutching his ankle. The ball lay inside the ropes, about a yard away, and the batsmen continued to run.

'Throw it in, you silly old git!' was one of the more printable shouts, as the batsmen crossed for a fourth run. Another player sped over and hurled the ball in as the batsmen calmly completed their fifth run and contemplated a sixth. Hugh was now rolling around the boundary in agony. He played no further part in the match and had to be helped up and escorted to the pavilion.

One hour later, after suffering a narrow defeat and carrying out a quick change, the team sat together in the changing room. We had driven over to Skipton in the school minibus and Al, who had drawn the short straw to be the designated driver, took charge of affairs.

'Right,' he said, 'as I see it, we have two options. Take Hugh to the hospital or go to the pub. How many people want to visit Skipton General?'

A forlorn hand went up from a red-faced Hugh.

'How many people think that the pub is a better option?'

A cheer went up as every other hand (some people raised both to make sure) shot into the air.

'Bastards!' said Hugh, weakly.

So there it was. We headed to the local, got Hugh to use two cricket bats as crutches to walk into the pub and supplied him with beer to numb the pain. We later returned to school, Hugh was driven home and then he attended his local hospital. It was confirmed that he had indeed broken his ankle.

Being 'designated driver' on one of the cricket trips was always a poisoned chalice and my worst experience was driving four players to and from York one year. One of the staff played regularly for a team in one of the York leagues and had arranged for us to play his mates at their base in the grounds of York Mental Hospital.

On arrival we were informed that there was ample time for a 'few pints' before the wickets were pitched and most of our staff needed no excuse. Their team also announced some changes to the usual format of matches, which they were entitled to do as the home team. They cancelled the need to retire after scoring twenty-five and insisted that players could bowl up to four overs, instead of everybody bowling two. Our skipper agreed to the terms and said we'd only use our best five bowlers to improve our chances of winning.

Three hours later we were back in the pub and most of our players were sampling the vast array of real ales on offer. I endured the diet coke, tonic water and blackcurrant and soda until closing time and then poured my four intoxicated team-mates into the car to start the long and noisy journey home. As for the match – we lost. I didn't get to bat, didn't get to bowl and during the opposition's twenty overs, I never touched the ball once. Cricket – what a cracking game it is.

Another favourite venue was one of the pitches in the centre of Pontefract Racecourse, where we played against teams from Featherstone, Castleford or Pontefract. On one occasion, the opposition's Head Teacher had gotten wind of the fixture and had offered his services as captain, as he had played second XI county cricket in his youth. Although he was once a talented player, he did little to endear himself to his staff, by altering the field after virtually every ball. They would respond to his orders with a 'Yes, Headmaster', but our batsmen in the middle could certainly hear other less pleasant responses as well. The teachers' mutterings were getting louder and louder after every unnecessary field change and it occurred to me that the head was either extremely hard-faced or hard of hearing.

On another occasion we played at the racecourse, the opposition fielded a Yorkshire League player, reputed to be a hard-hitting opening batsman. He was good, but nobody was more impressed with him than he was himself. After they won the toss and elected to bat, he told his skipper that he couldn't stay for the whole match, so would knock off his twenty-five runs in the first few overs and leave them to finish off. Sporting immaculate whites and what looked like a county cap, he sauntered nonchalantly to the crease, swigging from a can of Foster's. Having taken guard, he placed the opened can behind the stumps and surveyed the field placings, indicating with his bat where he intended to hit his first boundary.

Our opening bowler was Phil, a super-fit cyclist who had never played cricket before, but had been persuaded to 'give it a go.' He had tried to bowl a few overarm deliveries in the warm-up with very little speed or direction. At the umpire's signal, he started to trot into bowl, releasing the ball so early that it launched itself high (and I mean 'really high') into the sky. The cocky batsman had never seen anything like this before and lost sight of the ball in the bright sunshine, as it appeared to arc over his head. It did, but then started to come down from its terrific height to land squarely on the top of middle stump. The stump fell almost in slow motion to hit the can of lager, which emptied its contents with a satisfying 'glug, glug, glug.'

Everything seemed to stop for a few seconds as we looked on in disbelief. Soon the spell was broken - the batsman swore and his team mates on the boundary cheered and whooped in delight. As he walked away from the crease and we mobbed the shocked and stunned bowler, the wicketkeeper shouted,

'Oi, you've forgotten your drink!'

The batsman never turned round and scuttled away to the boundary. I've never seen a team more delighted to lose a wicket. As one of their players said at the end,

'Thanks for that. The guy's a tosser. He's always so full of himself, but I daresay we won't be hearing of any of his cricketing exploits for some considerable time!'

Rugby was also an important game at Horbury and in the old days we used to take a couple of coaches down to Wembley every year for the Challenge Cup Final. It didn't matter who was playing, we would get a block booking of tickets, even before the finalists were known. In those days we used to stand on the terraces at one end of the old stadium and once inside, students were free to go anywhere within the enclosure. It was always a crush - you never saw any of the students you were supposed to be supervising for a couple of hours, but there were never any issues. You arranged to meet them at a certain point inside the ground at the end of the presentations and lap of honour and once your group had re-assembled, you began the really difficult task of trying to find your coach amongst the hundreds of others in the coach park. On numerous occasions, it took us at least half an hour to find the coach and sometimes we had to send out search parties to find any missing groups lost in the maze of coaches and diesel fumes. There was only one occasion when we actually lost a child and of course, he was from my group. I'd met all of my students inside the ground as planned and had gotten them to follow me back to the coach in one line – you had to walk singly to get between all the coaches as they parked so close together. We eventually found the bus and I counted mine back on-board – one missing. I took a register to make sure and it was true – a fifth-form lad, reputed to be a bit of a 'hard man', was missing. He'd been with me in the stadium and certainly had entered the labyrinth of coaches. Three members of staff went out on search. We'd told students to stand between the 'twin towers' if ever they got lost – remember this was the 'old Wembley' and these were the days before mobile phones. No sign of him there. I went back in to a deserted Wembley to see if he had gone back in – another dead end. On the off-chance, one teacher went to the 'Missing Children's Office and lo and behold the tough-guy sixteen year old was found sitting on a chair and bawling his eyes out. They breed them tough at Horbury.

With such an interest in rugby league – many of the students played the game outside school and some even turned professional - you'd expect the school to coach a number of rugby league teams, but for some reason rugby union was the game of choice. In my first year of teaching, I was asked to take the first-year rugby team. Although I had no formal training (and absolutely no ability) in the sport, I was deemed safe enough to manage and coach a group of inexperienced and impressionable youngsters. Although two of the players had played the game before (one union and one league), most of them, like me, had absolutely no idea. After about five weeks of passing, tackling and learning some of the rules, it was arranged for us to play our first real game – an away fixture at a school in Barnsley the next Saturday morning.

The match was hardly a classic. Having accepted the warm welcome of some of the Barnsley players ('You're goin' home in a f**kin' ambulance') and cleared the pitch of broken glass, both teams strived to get more than two passes together and a half-time score line of 0-0 spoke volumes. The only real action was violence. Two Barnsley players started scrapping with each other after one lad had accused his team-mate of 'nipping' him in the lineout and then the referee slapped a Horbury player round the back of the head, after he'd kicked out against a Barnsley player who had punched him in the scrum. The Horbury player's father was standing next to me on the touchline and to my surprise barely raised an eyebrow. How times have changed. Towards the middle of the second half, we somehow managed to score a try under the posts and the one experienced union back slotted home the conversion. There was to be no further scoring in the match and after surviving a ruck which committed all fifteen Horbury players, I even took the risk of bringing on 'Tintin' on for the last few minutes and once he'd worked out which way we were playing, he was happy to run up and down as though he was making his international debut.

'Tintin' was the smallest of the players by at least a foot and unfortunately his lack of stature was not compensated by great wisdom or natural ability. He was once caught crying by a member of staff who asked what was wrong.

'It's the other kids, miss. They call me names to make fun of me,' he said.

'Well, Tintin isn't a bad nickname. He's the hero of a cartoon and you do look like him!'

'They don't call me 'Tintin' because I look like him. They call me 'Tintin' because I've got a small willy and when I get married, on our wedding night, my wife will say "T'int in, t'int in!"'

The teacher tried to stifle her laughter and moved on.

I think it was also 'Tintin' who was the star of another teacher's Sex Education lesson. The teacher had shown the first year boys the approved instructional video and then asked for any questions from students. He told them if they preferred anonymity, they could write down the questions on a piece of paper and place them in a box for answering next lesson. Alternatively, if they felt confident, they could raise a hand and he would answer the questions straight away. 'Tintin' was not too good at writing, so decided to brave it with a live question,

'Sir – you know when you do it?' he began nervously.

"You mean "make love,"' replied the teacher.

'Yeah! You are asleep, aren't you?!'

The Last of a Dying Breed?

In spite of all the changes that I have witnessed during my fifty year involvement with education, perhaps the biggest change of all is still to come. Many educationalists believe that the days of the classroom teacher are numbered and that the streamlined personal learning of the future will involve much more on-line content and flexible hours. They foresee students learning from behind a computer screen from a 'facilitator' who educates a class of thousands – indeed some Maths teachers in South Korea are already ploughing this fertile field, achieving 'rock star status' and making themselves millionaires in the process. Some believe that students will log on at home when they like and complete the set tasks at their own pace, whilst others predict a 'bring your own tech' scenario, with students still learning in the classroom environment, but using their own hardware to complete all proscribed tasks and to act as their 'text books.' The role of the teacher would be reduced to that of a trouble-shooter for the technology or a prison guard to assure compliance and deal with miscreants – probably students who have become weary of the impersonal nature of the new learning and are more engaged by the thrill of fidget spinners or flipping up a water bottle to get it to land in an upright position.

But will this 'non-teaching' really be the case? If you can now do complex calculations on your mobile phone and a computer can analyse huggings of data in a split second, what is the need for the teaching of Maths? I can recall the end of 'Maths-as-we-know-it' being predicted by some bright sparks once calculators were readily available in schools. I'm sure somebody said the same thing in the seventeenth century when William Oughtred came up with his idea for a slide rule or when John Napier decided log tables were the future. The truth is you have to know what to calculate and which data to use and analyse with your computer – the technology merely speeds up the process and is no substitute for 'mathematical understanding.'

You could say the same things about Modern Foreign Languages. If your mobile can act as a virtual translator of the spoken word and you can get an app to translate restaurant menus, will there ever be a need to 'parle français' or 'Deutsch sprechen' ever again? Of course, the answer is 'Yes.' Even in this post-Brexit world, the need to be able to speak a foreign language is essential. You can't point your device towards somebody speaking a strange language and slowly shout at them,

'Hold on old lad. The machine's working out what you're on about.'

You could probably find an argument for every subject in the curriculum and list ways in which technology could be used to replace traditional teaching. Take my own subject, History. The internet contains more than enough information to cover any area, time period or theme you could imagine. Logic would suggest that the future of History teaching would involve students using this fantastic resource to research their own areas of interest, yet this has been tried and set aside. 'Project-based learning' was seen as the future. Students would be encouraged to explore for themselves and would be able to apply the knowledge they acquired in some interesting format. Unfortunately, it was doomed to failure. The schools are at the mercy of the examination boards, who, in turn, kow-tow to the government. The new 'more rigorous' GCSE History (and all other subjects, for that matter) courses have removed all traces of opportunities for innovative research work or even continuous assessment at the government's behest and the new beefed-up syllabi and terminal examinations are much more based on memory-recall than they have been in the past. They are more a test of acquired factual knowledge than an application of such knowledge and as a result they have missed the golden opportunity to test the skills of the students rather than their short-term memories. Employers have been frequently complaining about the lack of skills of their new recruits for years, yet the new content-driven examinations merely seek to cram as much knowledge about Elizabethan England, the rise of Hitler or Medieval Medicine into the brains of the students. This short–term memory cramming serves no real purpose. A familiarity with the intricacies of the Ridolfi Plot, the Munich Putsch and Guy de Chauliac's work at the time of the Black Death is inconsequential. Even if the students could recall this acquired knowledge, it is difficult to envisage where it would be of any real use. As a result, it seems highly likely that would-be employers will bemoan the lack of skills for many years to come.

Ironically, at a time when testing is becoming more rigorous and the need for real 'subject specialists' would appear to be growing, education is staring into a financial abyss. Educational establishments everywhere are looking at ways of cutting their levels of expenditure, and expensive 'specialist ' teachers are one luxury that can be trimmed at a moment's notice. Teaching assistants do a great job and schools are looking to them to take on more responsibility and be in charge of teaching larger groups as solo teachers. (It also works out as a lot cheaper, but that could just be me being cynical.) In any case the curriculum is narrowing on a yearly basis – many subjects are being removed during Key Stage 3 and more time (and out-of-timetabled-hours Intervention time) is being hijacked for Maths and English. The broad and balanced curriculum that once contained Religious Education, Music, Drama and Technology is narrowing all the time and is tipped grossly in favour of the two key subjects, to the detriment of the education of the students. Even the Chief Inspector of OFSTED seems to agree. In her speech at the Festival of Education in June 2017, Amanda Spielman said, 'All children should study a broad and rich curriculum. Curtailing Key Stage 3 means prematurely cutting this off for children who may never have an opportunity to study some of these subjects again.'

Being a teacher of a subject outside the 'Big Two', can be a bit like feeling like a second-class citizen. Everything seems to stop for Maths and English. They get more curriculum time, much more money for resources and even eat into your own curriculum time. Some subjects are restrained from running after-school revision sessions on 'Maths and English evenings' and students can be withdrawn from your regular subject lesson for thirty or sixty minutes at a moments' notice, sometimes for a whole half-term, term or even year. Trying to teach a full GCSE with its recently dramatically increased content on two hours a week when four students are missing for the first half hour of the lesson and another three are missing for the second half, is nigh on an impossibility.

The scaling down and in some cases removal of these 'lesser' subjects could also result in some teachers being asked to teach outside their specialist areas and comfort zone. This has happened in the past of course, with mixed success. In my thirty four years at Horbury, I was timetabled to teach no fewer than seventeen different subjects – History, English, Integrated Humanities, Project Based Learning, School Based Curriculum, Latin, French, German, Religious Education, European Studies, Drama, Mathematics, Citizenship, Citizenship through History, Music, Lifeskills and Physical Education. This does not include the teaching requirements as part as a Form Teacher programme, such as Literacy, Numeracy and Personal, Social, Health and Careers Education. Suffice it to say, I was not exactly skilled in every subject – Grade C in GCE French at the age of 15 in 1975 did not prepare me adequately to teach Year 8 French for the whole of my second year of teaching, owing to a 'timetable error.' Still, I was probably better prepared than a hapless PE teacher in a local school who was forced into teaching a Year 7 English class for a couple of lessons a week to ensure that they were prepared for the future rigors of the new GCSE syllabus. Given Wilfred Owen's 'Dulce et decorum est' poem to introduce his class to the pleasures of war poetry, our friend told them that the poem was set in World War Two and the 'Dulce et decorum est' was a French phrase.

Another area that, in my opinion, needs to change for the future is that of observation and appraisal. Not content with the snapshot OFSTED reports, some Heads take it upon themselves to carry out 'MOCKSTEDS', departmental inspections, appraisal and learning walks (or 'learning stalks' as they are known by those at the chalkface). Sometimes they rely on their in-house management teams or buy in experts or so-called 'critical friends' to tell them what good Headteachers should already know.

I recall one such 'critical friend' being employed to scrutinise the Humanities department. His employment history proudly showed that he was a serving OFSTED inspector and regarded as ideally suited to carry out a rigorous testing of the Humanities department in an attempt to drive up standards. After deeper investigation, it was discovered that in the past he had been employed by a large Local Education Authority as a sort of 'raising standards guru'. Unfortunately a local newspaper suggested that he was told not to re-apply for his job as they alleged that standards had not been improved quickly enough. The teachers' favourite extension of the 'Those who can, do' adage to 'Those who can't teach, teach teachers' seems to be alive and well. His in-depth examination of my contribution towards the Humanities department consisted of a quick five-minute 'Learning Stalk' in one of my Year 11 GCSE History lessons. He uttered no words to me, engaged with no students and just picked up the exercise book of a student sitting near the front of the class. He had chosen one of my star students (who went on to achieve an A*) and after flicking through to see that the marking had been done throughout (the 'purple pen of progress'), I watched him read the latest piece of feedback on a set of exam questions completed as homework. He would have read, '20/20. Excellent detail, Dean and so much better than that awful John you sit next to.' He replaced the book and promptly left the room. If he'd bothered to check John's book, he'd have seen 'Full marks, John – you certainly put that upstart Dean in his place!' Whether this was acceptable or not, I do not know, because I received no feedback but the students who did get my feedback, loved it. Engagement and enjoyment are the keys to success. 'Banter for learning' – I tell you, it's the future!

Lesson observations can be haphazard too. I remember one member of the SLT watching the last half hour of a GCSE History lesson and berating me for not including a plenary. When I explained that by getting each of the thirty students in the last ten minutes of the lesson to explain orally a key feature about their learning in that lesson, I believed I'd covered that area, I was told it did not 'bring the lesson together enough.' I countered this with my argument that my plenary just got everybody to reflect on their learning and furthered their understanding and that plenaries did not have to be in any formulaic style, but this was met with just a shrug of the shoulders. At the end of the day it is just somebody's opinion, but it is human nature to prefer affirmation to criticism.

My most bizarre lesson observation happened a few years ago when an SLT member had arranged to see me teach a dodgy Y9 class after break one day. The class had some lively characters who could go from angels to devils at the flick of a switch. I knew that I'd have to be at my very best to escape unscathed. The lesson was planned with plenty of resources and I'd even prepared various tasks depending on the response of students to earlier tasks. I hoped that the observer would come in at the start of the lesson to give me a fighting chance – normally the Year 9's could be settled quickly in the first few minutes, but tended to get tired and fidgety the longer the lesson progressed. The starter was a slap-bang game with controlled audience participation. It went like a dream, enthused the students and was missed by the observer. The main part of the lesson was a round-the-room activity with students collecting key pieces of information and sharing it with group members. It was taking a big risk attempting group work with some of the Year 9's on this activity, but on this occasion they surprised me and worked extremely well. Still no sign of the observer. We were now into the second half of the lesson and the observer had to arrive at any second. The groups were to use written sources to further their understanding and then share their discoveries with the rest of the class in a plenary before writing a question to further their knowledge on a post-it note as an exit activity. All of this passed without interruption and a couple of lads even thanked me on the way out. I was still waiting. I went to see the 'inspector' who revealed that they'd forgotten about the whole thing. Apparently this was my fault because I should have left the class midway through to go to remind them. Anyway I passed over a copy of the lesson plan to show what they'd missed and two days later was handed a report that graded me 'satisfactory', with a couple of pointers on how to improve. I thought this was highly amusing - I think this 'distance learning' or 'non-threatening observation' could be the future. Other staff were outraged on my behalf – every teacher reacts differently and this leads us onto another future problem for many teachers – conformity and consistency.

Many schools, academies and trusts now seem to take delight in seeking advice, guidance and reassurance from educational partnership networks. Once again it's almost as if they don't trust their own instinct and prefer to access something that will provide them with a 'one-size-fits-all' solution. Of course, every school is different and every teacher even more so and it is for this reason that I believe such panaceas should be treated carefully. For example, a close friend at another school was given an exam by the Head Teacher that had been acquired from one of these 'network love-ins'. The teacher knew straight away that the questions were nothing like those set by the exam board of the syllabus his students were following – some of the subjects covered did not even exist in the course content. He pointed this out but was informed that although unfortunately no other school in the partnership network actually followed the same syllabus, or even exam board, the Head Teacher had been assured that the exam would be fine for their students. Accordingly, the exam was set, the students struggled (especially with the topics they were not required to study) and when the poor results of the 'pre-public examination', were circulated, the Head Teacher put my hapless friend on 'capability'. Can you believe it?! (Ironically the teacher was exonerated when a 'critical friend' was purchased by the school to carry out a 'MOCKSTED' of his department. He was found to be a really good teacher and the only criticism came in of his choice of 'pre-public examination' materials – I tell you, you couldn't make this up.)

Of course, the last story is an extreme case, but the fact that every school, teacher, and for that matter, student is different, means that taking a 'one-size-fits-all' solution is never going to work. Having proscribed lessons that every single teacher is to follow to the letter is a recipe for disaster and does not take into account the comparative strengths and weaknesses of the school, teacher or student. You can't help but stifle creativity and spontaneity if every single teacher is to teach in the same manner, using the same worksheet.

One 'partnership' suggested teaching everything at Key Stage 3 in six-week blocks, even if subjects were only time-tabled for one lesson per week. Lesson 1 would contain a baseline assessment test to check on prior knowledge and Lesson 6 would be a standard test for all students to check progress (or lack of) – in other words, some subjects would spend a third of their curriculum time engaged in testing. When a colleague questioned the wisdom of testing students at the start and end of the module with the same tests for each student, she was met with a shrug of the shoulders. She pointed out that she'd spent hours during her training and years of practice creating differentiated materials and had used a plethora of differentiation strategies in an attempt to engage students of all abilities and help them to succeed. She wanted to know how differentiation would 'fit in' with this new system. The senior leader in charge of promoting the partnership's doctrine was crystal clear on this and pointed out that differentiation was unnecessary – he confessed that he had only ever used differentiation twice in his entire career and it had not held him back. Once again, something that had been seen as central to good practice over a number of years is swept aside without a second glance.

In spite of his certainty, I am convinced that the future of teaching is based not on uniformity and standardised worksheets, but rather on creativity and engagement. Nobody is going to look back on their education and say,

'Ooh! I remember that lesson when we had that beautifully-produced standardised worksheet. I loved filling in the table and the missing words exercise and as for the highlighting activity........'

Students are much more likely to remember the good stories, humour and above all, banter. It's a fact that many students are much more able to recall the throwaway remarks and snippets of information that the teacher has forgotten about as soon as they've said it, rather than swathes of important subject matter.

A classic example happened to me a good few years ago. A young man presented himself at the school and asked if he could speak to any staff who might remember him from his time at school, five years before. The receptionist checked on the list of staff scheduled to be free at that time and her eyes alighted on my name. I was called to the reception and met face-to-face a student I instantly recognised as one of the most challenging History students I'd ever encountered. He'd somehow managed to get a 'D' in his GCSE History, which was his highest grade. I shook his hand warmly (thinking inside how there had been times when I'd rather have shaken his neck) and we walked down to my classroom. He told me about his life after school – he'd worked full-time in a shop and after a few months had started to hate it. He realised that he'd wasted his time at school, but was determined to improve his prospects. He had enrolled in night school to get his GCSE's in the basic subjects (not History) and then moved onto college to study A-levels. The whole process had taken five years since leaving the school and he had just been accepted at a university to study for a science degree. He was going to be starting university at the same time as his little sister, three years his junior.

'I was a nob when I was at school, Sir. Wasn't I?'

'Well, I wouldn't go as far as that!' (actually, I would – he was a bit of a bell-end)

'I never listened. You always said I was wasting my time and would regret it one day. You were right. I'll always remember one thing you said that I'll never forget. . .'

(I was hooked. This was to be one of those career-defining moments in a teacher's life when you can bask in the glory when you realise that one of your pieces of advice has sunk in and really made a difference to someone's future)

'You said that Les Ferdinand would play for England and you were right!'

Yes, you read it correctly. My comment about Les Ferdinand when he was starting to play regularly at Queens' Park Rangers was the one thing that he'd remembered. Never mind my words of wisdom about how to get on in life or any of the content from two years of GCSE History, my lasting contribution in someone's life is a prediction about a young footballer who would go on to represent his country. My moment of glory would have to wait for a few years.

It was worth the wait though. In my final year of teaching, I received my career-defining moment. It came in an email sent to the school and directed onto me. It was a letter from an ex-student, John, who had gone on to become a very successful History teacher in London:

"Dear Mr. Matthews,

Being an awkward teenager I don't think I expressed this very well at the time, but I would like to thank you for the enthusiasm and dedication you showed in teaching me History during my time at Horbury. Lessons were fun and I can still remember facts about Galen, listening to 'Sunday Bloody Sunday' and Ian Paisley's 'triumphalism' ten years later. . . . . .

However, when I graduated I wasn't sure what I wanted to 'do', as they say. After quite a bit of soul searching I remembered something that you had said. You said that of all your friends from university, you were paid the least, but that you were the happiest. I thought that was definitely the kind of philosophy that I could buy into and it is something that I continue to try and live by. I decided to volunteer in a local school and immediately knew that I was in the right place. . . .

I wanted to tell you this in order to thank you. When I think about the kind of teacher that I am, the kind of teacher that I continue to aspire to be, I think of your classes. From impersonating Leonid Brezhnev to making jokes about Gustav Stresemann (don't stress, man!) I continue to be inspired by the way that you engage your students."

Wow! What a fabulous letter to receive. At first, after admittedly shedding a few tears, I just felt sheer contentment. Then, after reading it a few more times, I realised that John had summed up what is really important in education to me – enthusiasm and engagement achieved through banter. This is not something I invented or purposefully developed – it just happened and it happens to probably every other teacher. Every teacher who has succeeded in engaging students by building a rapport with them deserves to have a letter like this, so if you are reading this and recall a teacher who inspired you but you never told them, let them know now. Write them a letter, send an email, phone them up, use social media or whatever – but please, just tell them. Do it as soon as you finish reading this; don't put it off or you'll never get round to doing it.

It seems to be the natural place to end the book. Go out at the top. The fifty years have flown by and as I take up full retirement, I look back fondly (and admittedly sometimes through rose-tinted glasses) at my time within the education system. I'll miss the students, I'll miss my colleagues, but above all, I'll miss the banter.

Thank you for reading this book.